Principles Of
FAMILY LIFE

Principles Of
FAMILY LIFE

Dick Iverson
with
**Kevin Conner,
Rick Johnston, Ken Malmin,
Bill Scheidler and Wendell Smith.**

BIBLE TEMPLE PUBLISHING
7545 N.E. GLISAN • PORTLAND, OR. 97213
(503) 253-9020

PRINCIPLES OF FAMILY LIFE

Available from:

BIBLE TEMPLE PUBLISHING
9200 NE FREMONT
PORTLAND, OREGON 97220
(503) 253-9020 • (800) 777-6057

ISBN 0-914936-35-2
Printed in U.S.A.

Principles Of
FAMILY LIFE

Table of Contents

Foreword

In a recent publication, a Catholic priest commented on ineffective Christian education. He said, "The long-range solution is solid investment in the Christian education of parents". Over the years of our ministry, we have grown in our awareness of the needs of the Christian home. The Christian home is really the foundation of the Church. As the family goes, so goes the Church. Consequently the Church around the world is recognizing the need to build Christian character and righteousness into both parents and children.

Almost every major Christian education publisher is now designing curriculum materials that attempt to implement truth and teaching on the home level. The Christian book market has been flooded with books on the family and the home, and cassette tape albums on the subject abound. We are living in a generation where this widespread emphasis on the family is both needed and welcomed.

In the past few years, God has been speaking to us about the needed balance between the Church and the home. We recognize that the Church is "the pillar and ground of the truth" (I Timothy 3:15), and that God's people are to continue "steadfastly in the apostles' doctrine" (Acts 2:42). Yet, truth and doctrine are to be worked out from "house to house" (Acts 2:46) and by teaching our children "diligently" during the daily processes of life (Deuteronomy 6:4-9).

Several years ago, we wrote a notebook entitled, *Principles of Church Life.* This notebook has been used as a six month instructional transition for those desiring to become members of our local church. It has been quite successful for us. As a sequel to this course, we are presenting the *Principles of Family Life* Notebook. We believe that this course is vital to the continued growth of our people as a "family church", and that this notebook will be an ongoing and useful tool in our people's homes.

I want to express my appreciation to the fine team of staff members who worked together in writing and designing this notebook. We trust that it will be a blessing to you and to your family, and that it will become a real strength and help in your home.

K.R. "Dick" Iverson
Pastor
Bible Temple
Portland, Oregon

1

Definition and Purpose of the Family

SCRIPTURE READING: Deuteronomy 6

SHOULD THE FAMILY BE A VERY IMPORTANT STRUCTURE IN OUR DAY

YES!

The home or family is the basic unit of all of society. The family is to society what the atom is to the universe. It is the cornerstone on which everything is built. Any society that allows the family unit to collapse, will itself eventually collapse. This is demonstrated vividly throughout history. The most classic example is that of the Roman empire.

Gibbon in his classic work entitled "The Decline and Fall of the Roman Empire" lists five main rains for the fall of Rome. The first reason that he gives is the undermining of the dignity and the sanctity of the home.

The following is an historical excerpt which describes part of the family condition in the period of the Roman Republic about seventy-seven to sixty BC:

The increase of wealth conspired with the corruption of politics to loosen morals and the marriage bond. Despite increasing competition from women and men, prostitution continued to flourish; brothels and the taverns that usually housed them were so popular that some politicians organized votes through the . . . guild of brothelkeepers. Adultery was so common as to attract little attention unless played up for political purposes, and practically every well-to-do woman had at least one divorce. This was not the fault of women; it resulted largely from the subordination of marriage, in the upper classes, to money and politics. Men chose wives, or youths had wives chosen for them, to get a rich dowry or make advantageous connections . . . Such unions were "marriages de politique"; as soon as their utility ended, the husband looked for another wife as a steppingstone to higher place or greater wealth. He did not need to give a reason; he merely sent his wife a letter announcing her freedom and his. Some men did not marry at all, alleging distaste for the forwardness and extravagance of the new woman; many lived in free unions with concubines or slaves . . .

Under these circumstances women . . . [began] looking lightly upon their marriage vows and seeking in liaisons the romance or affection that political matrimony had failed to bring. There was, of course, a majority of good women, even among the rich; but a new freedom was breaking down the . . . ancient family discipline. Roman women now moved about almost as freely as men. They dressed in diaphanous silks from India and China, and ransacked Asia for perfumes and jewelry. Marriage "cum manu" [with continuance] disappeared, and women divorced their husbands as readily as men their wives. A growing proportion of women sought expression in cultural pursuits: they learned Greek, studied philosophy, wrote poetry, gave public lectures, played, sang, and danced, and opened literary "salons"; some engaged in businesses; a few practiced medicine or law." (The Story of Civilization, Volume III, Caesar and Christ, Will Durant, Simon and Schuster, New York, 1944, 134-135)

As in the natural, even so in the spiritual. If the home is vital to the success of a society, it is even more important for the success of the Church. To establish a new home is the reason that a man leaves his father and his mother *(Genesis 2:24)*.

WHAT IS A GOOD DEFINITION OF THE FAMILY?

There are several ways of looking at the family.

— English Dictionary
An English dictionary defines the family as:

* A group of persons of common ancestry;
* A group of persons living under one roof and usually under one head;
* A group of things related by common characteristics and properties;
* The basic unity of society having as its nucleus, two adults living together and cooperating in the care and rearing of their own or adopted children.

While this definition is good, we must also understand the biblical concept of the family.

— The Old Testament
In the Old Testament, the family was a very close unit. The family structure itself was the vehicle through which God communicated to man *(Genesis 7:1, 7, 13 cf. 6:18; 49:1, 2)*.

The concept of menial labor and service is found in the origin of the words that are rendered "family" in the Old Testament. Therefore, the family involves work.

— The New Testament
In the New Testament several words are used for "family" or "household". The most enlightening of these is the word "therapeia". This word is a very versatile word and has quite a range of meanings depending on the context. It is therefore translated in the following ways in the Bible and extra-biblical sources:

* Household *(Matthew 24:45)*
* Servants *(Luke 12:42, NAS)*
* Healing *(Luke 9:11; Revelation 22:2)*
* Worship of God (extra-biblical sources)
* Service (extra-biblical sources)

The verb form of this word means "to serve; to care for; to care".

The family, therefore, is to be a base where work, care, service, healing, and worship are common elements.

WHAT IS THE PURPOSE OF THE FAMILY?

When God created and ordained the family, He did not do so without purpose or design. God established the family as a context in which man would realize the eternal purposes of divine image and dominion for which he was created *(Genesis 1:26-28)*. The family is therefore a God-ordained context for the establishment and development of:

* God-centered relationships and fellowship
* God-like character
* God-ordained ministry and function
* Natural and spiritual reproduction
* Spiritual and natural dominion

It is in the family that the true principles of relationship to God and to man are laid down. It is in the family that true God-like character will be produced *(II Timothy 1:5)*. It is in the family that all ministry and function will be tested and proven) *(I Timothy 3:4, 5; 5:4; Titus 2:5)*. It is through the ministry of the family that the family of God will be enlarged.

WHAT ARE SOME BIBLICAL EXAMPLES THAT SHOW THE IMPORTANCE OF THE FAMILY?

In the Bible there are both positive and negative examples of family life. God expects us to follow the positive examples. He also wants us to be warned by and to learn from the negative examples *(I Corinthians 10:6, 11, 18A)*.

Positive Examples:

* Joshua:
  Joshua said, ". . . as for me and my house, we will serve the Lord" *(Joshua 24:15)*.

* Abraham:
  God said, "For I have chosen him, in order that he may command his children and his household after him to keep the way of the Lord by doing righteousness and justice; in order that the Lord may bring upon Abraham what He has spoken about him" *(Genesis 18:19)*.

* Job:
  "There was a man in the land of Uz, whose name was Job . . . and seven sons and three daughters were born to him . . . and his sons used to go and hold a feast in the house of each one on his day . . . and it came about, when the days of feasting had completed their cycle, that Job would send and consecrate them, rising up early in the morning and offering burnt offerings ac-

cording to the number of them all; for Job said, 'Perhaps my sons have sinned and cursed God in their hearts.' Thus Job did continually" *(Job 1:1, 2, 4, 5)*.

• Cornelius:

"Now there was a certain man at Caesarea named Cornelius . . . a devout man, and one who feared God with all his household . . . [who said] 'Now then [Peter], we are all here present before God to hear all that you have been commanded by the Lord'" *(Acts 10:1, 2, 33)*.

• The Philippian Jailor:

"And they [Paul and Silas] spoke the word of the Lord to him together with all who were in his house . . . and immediately he was baptized, he and all his household . . . having believed in God with his whole household" *(Acts 16:31-34)*.

• Crispus:

"And Crispus, the leader of the synagogue, believed in the Lord with all his household . . ." *(Acts 18:8)*.

• Timothy, Lois and Eunice:

"For I am mindful of the sincere faith within you, which first dwelt in your grandmother Lois, and your mother Eunice, and I am sure that it is in you as well" *(II Timothy 1:5)*.

Negative Examples:

• Eli:

"For I [the Lord] have told him [Eli] that I am about to judge his house forever for the iniquity which he knew, because his sons brought a curse upon themselves and he did not rebuke them" *(I Samuel 3:13)*.

• Samuel:

"His [Samuel's] sons, however, did not walk in his ways, but turned aside after dishonest gain and took bribes and perverted justice" *(I Samuel 8:3)*.

• A Family with Hatred:

"Better is a dish of vegetables where love is, than a fattened ox and hatred with it" *(Proverbs 15:17)*.

• A Family with an Offended Brother:

"A brother offended is harder to be won than a strong city, and contentions are like the bars of a castle" *(Proverbs 18:19)*.

• A Family with a Foolish Son:

"A foolish son is destruction to his father . . ." *(Proverbs 19:13A)*.

• A Family with an Argumentative Wife:

". . . the contentions of a wife are a constant dripping" *(Proverbs 19:13B)*, and it is better to live in a corner of the roof than in a house shared with a contentious woman" *(21:9, 19; 25:24)*.

WHAT IS OUR WORKING DEFINITION OF THE FAMILY?

The family is the God-ordained basic unit of society having parental headship and discipline which is established for the purpose of enjoying a common life together through working, caring, sharing, serving and ministering to God, to others, and to itself.

FAMILY • PROJECTS •

SECTION 1
LESSON 1
"Definition and Purpose of the Family"

"And these words which I command thee this day, shall be in thine heart: And thou shalt teach them diligently unto thy children and shalt talk of them when thou sittest in thine house, and when thou walkest by the way; and when thou liest down, and when thou risest up"
(Deuteronomy 6:6,7).

Project One ☐ Have a discussion time with your family and have every family member write down their own definition of a family. Have the small children draw pictures of a family. Discuss these definitions and talk about how your family could be better. Perhaps, give a prize for the best definition or picture. Or, give a family prize for everybody. Have a family celebration!

DATE ATTEMPTED: _____

RESULTS: _____

_____

_____

_____

Project Two ☐ Read each of the positive and negative examples of families from this lesson and discuss why each family situation was good or bad. Or, draw a poster listing the good and bad qualities.

DATE ATTEMPTED: _____

RESULTS: _____

_____

_____

_____

The Need for Restoration in the Family

SCRIPTURE READING: Genesis 1-4

WHAT HAPPENED TO MANKIND IN THE BEGINNING THAT MAKES AN EMPHASIS ON THE FAMILY SO NECESSARY?

Sin in each family member!

When Adam and Eve fell into sin, the first family lost God's image. Man and woman, who had been in perfect harmony with the ways of God, crossed God's will and separated themselves from God. The following things happened to man when he fell:

- Man became a sinner *(Psalm 51:5).*
- Man's mind became defiled *(Titus 1:15; Colossians 1:21; Romans 8:5-8).*
- Man became a slave to sin *(Romans 6:17).*
- Man became an enemy of God *(James 4:4).*
- Man became dead in trespasses and sins *(Ephesians 2:1, 2).*
- Man began a course to eternal damnation *(II Thessalonians 1:6-10).*

Because of his sin, man does not know the ways of God. The ways of God are foolishness to him. He cannot know them. What seems right to man only produces death *(I Corinthians 2:14; Proverbs 14:12).*

HOW DID ADAM'S FALL AFFECT EACH MEMBER OF OUR FAMILY?

When Adam fell, we all fell, for we were born in him *(Romans 5:12).* After Adam fell, he no longer reproduced in his family members the image and likeness of God. Instead, he reproduced his own fallen image and likeness in all of his children including all of us. *(Genesis 5:1-13; Romans 5:18, 19).*

WHAT EFFECT DID SIN HAVE ON FAMILY LIFE?

Sin produced the following family problems:

— Disrespect for and rebellion against parental authority:

- Ham showed disrespect for his father Noah by not covering him with a garment *(Genesis 9:20-27).*
- Rachel rebelled against her father Laban by stealing the household idols *(Genesis 31:19).*
- Reuben insulted God and his father by lying with his father Jacob's concubines *(Genesis 35:22).*

— Hatred and envy among family members:

- Cain killed Abel because God accepted Abel's offering but did not accept his own *(Genesis 4:1-8)*.

- Esau bore a grudge against Jacob because Esau sold his brithright to him for some pottage *(Genesis 25:29-34; 27:41)*.

- Josephs's brethren were jealous of him because he had a dream that they would bow down to him *(Genesis 37:11)*.

— Improper and unprincipled relationships in marriage:

- Lamech committed polygamy by taking both Adah and Zillah as his wives *(Genesis 4:19)*.

- *The sons of God took whomever they pleased of the daughters of men to be their wives (Genesis 6:1-7)*.

- Lot drank wine and committed incest with his two daughters *(Genesis 19:30-38)*.

— Self-centeredness and dishonesty in marriage:

- Both Abraham and Isaac said that their wives were their sisters in order to protect themselves while exposing their wives to adulterous situations *(Genesis 12:10-20; 26:7-16)*.

— A lack of respect and love for children on the part of parents and relatives:

- Lot offered his two virgin daughters to a city of sodomites *(Genesis 19:8)*.

- Laban, Jacob's uncle, gave him, at the first, the opposite daughter that he was expecting to marry *(Genesis 29:18-30)*.

— Husbands and wives having divided interests:

- Lot's wife turned back from her husband to look again at Sodom and therefore became a pillar of salt *(Genesis 19:26)*.

- Isaac loved his son Esau, whereas, Rebekah loved Jacob *(Genesis 25:28)*.

— Wives usurping their husbands authority through deceptive means:

- Rebekah disguised her favorite son, Jacob, to look like Esau in order to deceive Isaac, her husband *(Genesis 27:5-17)*.

— Parents favoring one child over another child:

- Isaac loved Esau, whereas, Rebekah loved Jacob *(Genesis 25:28)*.

- Jacob's favorite son was Joseph because he was the son of his old age *(Genesis 37:3)*.

— Unfaithfulness between husbands wives:

- Potiphar's wife tried to seduce Joseph into an adulterous relationship *(Genesis 39:7)*.

— A lack of proper parental discipline of children:

- Eli, the priest, did not rebuke his sons for their sins of immorality and injustice *(I Samuel 3:11-14)*.

- Samuel, the prophet, did not raise his sons properly. Instead, his sons turned aside to dishonest gain, bribes, and perversions of justice *(I Samuel 8:1-5)*.

The family, which began as God's vehicle for the development of relationship, character, ministry, and fruitfulness in man, was rendered ineffective by the introduction of sin.

WHAT IS GOD'S ANSWER TO ALL OF THESE FAMILY PROBLEMS?

God's answer is Calvary, the place where Jesus died on the cross for all of men's sins. Through the cross, God restores not only the inward spirit of man. He also redeems every area of man's life including the family. God is not just interested in restoring individuals or restoring the church, God also desired to restore the home *(Jeremiah 30:3, 20; 31:1, 13. Malachi 4:4-6; Luke 1:17)*.

- The house of Cornelius believed in Jesus together *(Acts 10:1-2; 44-48)*.
- The house of Lydia had all been water baptized *(Acts 16:14-15)*.
- The Philippian jailor's whole household believed in Jesus and was water baptized *(Acts 16:31-34)*.

WHAT IS MAN'S RESONSIBILITY IN GOD'S RESTORATION OF THE HOME?

Man must obey whatever God's Word says about the role of husbands, fathers, wives, mothers and children. Because man's understanding is darkened, he has strayed from God's truth concerning the home. Only the Word of God can direct him to God's pattern for the Christian family. God has done His part in sending Christ to save each individual family member and give the grace to contribute to their family as His Word commands.

— Man, therefore, must:

- Repent of his sins against God and his other family members;
- Receive Christ as the Lord of his life and of his family;
- Search the Scriptures for the truth about his God-ordained role in his family;
- Practice his God-ordained family role daily.

Through these ways, God will restore the home to its original beauty and function that He intended.

• FAMILY PROJECTS •

SECTION 1
LESSON 2
"The Need for Restoration in the Family"

"And these words which I command thee this day, shall be in thine heart: And thou shalt teach them diligently unto thy children and shalt talk of them when thou sittest in thine house, and when thou walkest by the way; and when thou liest down, and when thou risest up"
(Deuteronomy 6:6, 7).

Project One ☐ Make a list of the specific problems that occur in your home. Discuss how these are caused by sin and selfishness. List problems such as: arguing, disobedience, anger, and unfairness. Then ask, "Why do these happen?"

DATE ATTEMPTED: _____

RESULTS: _____

_____

_____

_____

Project Two ☐ Make a chart together of the four steps involved in man's responsibility in the restoration of the home as given in this lesson. Attempt to solve at least one specific problem in your home by applying the four steps to the situation.

DATE ATTEMPTED: _____

RESULTS: _____

_____

_____

The Heavenly Family

SCRIPTURE READING: *Ephesians 3:14-15*
(see *The Amplified New Testament*)

WHERE DID THE CONCEPT OF THE FAMILY ORIGINATE?

The concept of the family originated with God. All Biblical theology can be traced back to God Himself. Everything originates in God. The original and pattern family is that which is illustrated and demonstrated in the very nature and being of God. The Scriptural revelation of the eternal Godhead is that of the Father, the Son, and the Holy Spirit *(Matthew 28:19; II Corinthians 13:14)*.

WHAT TWO ASPECTS DO THE SCRIPTURES INDICATE ARE INCLUDED IN THE CONCEPT OF THE HEAVENLY FAMILY?

The two Scriptural aspects of the Heavenly Family are: "The Godhead Family" as revealed in the Father, the Son, and the Holy Spirit and "The Angelic Family" as revealed in the heavenly angels which God created.

SPECIFICALLY, HOW DO THE SCRIPTURES REVEAL THE CONCEPT OF THE HEAVENLY FAMILY IN THE GODHEAD?

This family concept is revealed in the triune nature and being of God: the Father, the Son and the Holy Spirit.

The Father:

The Old Testament reveals the fatherhood of God in the following Scriptures:

- "Do you thus repay the Lord, O foolish and unwise people? Is not He your Father who has bought you? He has made you and established you" *(Deuteronomy 32:6)*.

- "Sing to God, sing praises to His name . . . A father of the fatherless and a judge for the widows, Is God in His holy habitation. God makes a home for the lonely . . . *(Psalm 68:4-6)*.

- "I have found David My servant . . . He will cry to Me, 'Thou art my Father, My God, and the rock of my salvation'" *(Psalm 89:20, 26)*.

- "Just as a father has compassion on his children, So the Lord has compassion on those who fear Him" *(Psalm 103:13)*.

- Other passages include: *Proverbs 3:12; Isaiah 9:6; 63:16; 64:8; Jeremiah 3:4, 19; Malachi 1:6; 2:10.*

The New Testament also reveals the fatherhood of God.

The New Testament gives us a great revelation of the father heart of God. Jesus especially came to reveal this concept to us *(Matthew 6:8-15; Luke 11:1-4)*. God is the Father of all men only in the sense that He created all men and gave them natural birth. God, however, only becomes the Father of men in the sense of having them as children in His family by men personally receiving spiritual birth through Jesus Christ *(John 3:1-5; II Corinthians 6:17-18)*.

In his epistles, the apostle Paul delights to speak continually of "God our Father" *(I Corinthians 1:3; II Corinthians 1:2; Galatians 1:3; Ephesians 1:2; 3:14-15)*.

A study of God shows the true characteristics of a father. A father's love, concern, provision, protection, authority, and strength are all seen in Him. These characteristics are the same qualities that God desires to be in all earthly fathers. Our heavenly Father is the ideal father after whom all earthly fathers should seek to pattern themselves.

The Son:

Jesus, the eternal Son of God, becomes "the pattern Son" in the Godhead family. Both Old and New Testament speak of His Sonship.

- Several Old Testament Scriptures speak of His Sonship: *Psalm 2:7, 12; Proverbs 30:1-4; Isaiah 7:14; 9:6-9.*

- The New Testament abounds with the revelation of the Son of God, the WORD made flesh *(John 1:14-18; 3:16)*. The Son of God became the Son of Man by the virgin birth that the sons of men might become the sons of God by new birth *(John 3:1-16)*. The Father testified to His "Beloved Son" while here on earth, thus revealing His perfect obedience to His Father's will *(Matthew 3:17; 17:1-5; 2 Peter 1:16-19; John 17:1-5)*.

- A study of the Lord Jesus Christ, God the Son, shows the true nature and characteristics of an ideal Son. The qualities of total dependence, submission, and unquestioning obedience to the Father's will exemplify characteristics that every child of God should have. Chris is indeed "the pattern Son".

The Holy Spirit:

Although the Scriptures speak of the Father, Son, and Holy Spirit in the masculine gender, and although traditionally we do not usually ascribe femininity to any of the three divine persons, the following Scriptures do attribute the qualities of womanhood and motherhood to God the Holy Spirit. (These references, however, should not be taken out of their Scriptural context.)

Characteristics of an Earthly Mother or Woman:
- She broods over her young.

Characteristics of the Holy Spirit:
- He brooded over the chaotic waters before God's Word brought order *(Genesis 1:1, 2)*.

Characteristics of an Earthly Mother or Woman:
- She comforts her young.

Characteristics of the Holy Spirit:
- He is called the Comforter *(John 16:7 KJV)*, and God said in *Isaiah 66:12, 13*, ". . . you shall be nursed. . . as one whom his mother comforts, so I will comfort you . . ."

Characteristics of an Earthly Mother or Woman:
- She gives her breasts to her young for their physical nourishment and strength.

Characteristics of the Holy Spirit:
- He is alluded to as providing spiritual nourishment and strength to believers in the meaning of one of the names of God, El Shaddai. El (God) means, "The Strong One". Shaddai means, "The Breasted One" from 'shad' (breast: *Genesis 49:25; John 3:12; Psalm 22:9; Song of Solomon 1:13; 4:5; Isaiah 28:9)*. Therefore, El Shaddai means, "The Strong and Breasted One".

Characteristics of an Earthly Mother or Woman:
- She is known as having similar characteristics to that of a dove *(Song of Solomon 1:15; 2:14; 4:1; 5:2, 12; 6:9)*.

Characteristics of the Holy Spirit:
- He is symbolized as a dove in the New Testament *(Matthew 3:16; Mark 1:10; Luke 3:22; John 1:32)*.

Characteristics of an Earthly Mother or Woman:
- She gives birth to natural children.

Characteristics of the Holy Spirit:
- He gives birth to spiritual children who are "born of the Spirit" *(John 3:5, 6, 8)*.

Characteristics of an Earthly Mother or Woman:
- She is fruitful in her producing of children.

Characteristics of the Holy Spirit:
- He is fruitful in His producing divine character qualities in believers called, "the fruit of the Spirit" *(Galatians 5:22, 23)*.

Characteristics of an Earthly Mother or Woman:
- She is a servant to her household *(Proverbs 31:27)*.

Characteristics of the Holy Spirit:
- He is the servant person to the Godhead *(Genesis 24:2-4, typologically)* who serves only to have all glory be given to the Son *(John 16:14)*.

Thus, the concept of the family had its origin in the Godhead. The Triune God has demonstrated in His own nature and being the ideal family. All of the qualities of the Godhead Family should be manifested in the earthly family.

The Godhead Family (Father, Son, and Holy Spirit) correspond to the earthly family (father, son, and mother). The presence of all three personages in the Godhead completes the triunity that constitutes a family.

DID GOD CREATE A HEAVENLY BEYOND THAT WHICH IS FAMILY DEMONSTRATED IN HIS OWN BEING?

Yes! God created the angelic family. The Father, Son, and Holy Spirit were not content to dwell in eternity as an isolated or selfish family. The father heart of God longed for a vast family of sons and daughters who would conform in character and loving obedience to His own eternal Son. Hence, God created the angelic hosts. These angelic hosts were created as spirit beings, like God's spirit *(John 4:22-24)*. Angels are also spoken of as being "sons of God" *(Job 1:6; 2:1; 38:7; cf. Isaiah 14:12)*. However, angels were not begotten sons but created sons *(Hebrews 1:4-5)*.

WHY DID GOD CREATE THE ANGELS?

God created the angels for several reasons.

- He created the angels to be His sons. God is and desires to have a family as every earthly father does.

- He created the angels to be creatures that would please Him. *(Revelation 4:11)*.

- He created the angels to be ministering the servants to do His will *(Psalm 104:4; Hebrews 1:6, 7)*.

- He created the angels to be worshippers *(Rev. 5:11-14)*.

DID GOD HAVE ANY REBELLION FROM THIS ANGELIC FAMILY?

Yes! Certain angels rose up in rebellion and self-will against God. They brought disruption and chaos to the angelic family. These angels are spoken of as fallen angels or "the angels which sinned" *(II Peter 2:4; KJV; Jude 6; cf. I Corinthians 11:10)*. Sin will destroy any family.

WHAT DID GOD THE FATHER DO ABOUT THIS REBELLION?

The Scriptures show us that God exercised divine discipline against these rebel angels. He judged them and cast them out of heaven. In due time they will have a final trial and then be cast into the lake of fire *(II Peter 2:4; Jude 6; Matthew 25:41; Revelation 20:11-15)*.

DID ALL THE ANGELS REBEL AGAINST GOD THE FATHER?

No! Not all of the angels rebelled. There were angels who remained true to God and submitted their free wills to His loving and supreme will.

These angels are called "the elect angels" *(I Timothy 5:21)*. God rewarded these angels with a perfection from which it is impossible to fall. The elect angels have the qualities of being perfectly obedient sons of God.

IS IT GOD'S INTENTION TO REPLACE THESE FALLEN ANGELS?

Yes! God's intention is to replace these fallen angels with another family. This family is His redeemed earthly family the Church. It was for this reason that God created a NEW family, the earthly family. This is seen in God's purpose in the Garden of Eden when He created Adam and Eve. Man was created "a little lower than the angels *(Psalm 8:5A)*. God's desire and intention is to have a vast family of sons and daughters who are conformed to the image of His Son Jesus Christ *(Romans 8:29-30)*.

It is for this reason that Paul speaks of "every family in heaven and in earth" *(Ephesians 3:15)*. The Heavenly Family is seen in the Godhead Family and then in the Angelic Family. The next section will show us the Earthly Family.

FAMILY PROJECTS •

SECTION 1
LESSON 3
"The Heavenly Family"

"And these words which I command thee this day, shall be in thine heart: And thou shalt teach them diligently unto thy children and shalt talk of them when thou sittest in thine house, and when thou walkest by the way; and when thou liest down, and when thou risest up"
(Deuteronomy 6:6,7).

Project One

☐ Discuss the principles and Scriptures given in this lesson as to how the Godhead (Father, Son, and Holy Spirit) is like a family (father, child, mother). Try to make it as simple and as practical as possible.

DATE ATTEMPTED: _____

RESULTS: _____

_____

_____

_____

Project Two

☐ Tell your family the story of God's first family (the Angelic Family) using the ideas from this lesson as your source and guide. Relate the lessons learned from that first family to how your own family can serve the Lord.

DATE ATTEMPTED: _____

RESULTS: _____

_____

_____

_____

4

SECTION I — CONCEPTS OF THE FAMILY

The First Earthly Family

SCRIPTURE READING: Genesis 1 and 2

WHAT DOES THE FIRST EARTHLY FAMILY OF ADAM AND EVE TEACH US ABOUT THE PURPOSE OF GOD?

The first earthly family teaches us that God's plan and purpose is based on divine grace and not on human works *(Genesis 1:1; 2:7)*. God was going to take some of the insignificant dust of the ground and use it for a great purpose.

It also teaches us that God has chosen to accomplish His great purpose by using human channels *(Genesis 1:26-28)*.

It also teaches us that God's plan and purpose was to be demonstrated in and through the family. Adam alone could never have fulfilled God's ultimate purpose *(Genesis 2:18; 1:28)*.

WHAT WERE THE CHARGES GIVEN TO THE FIRST EARTHLY FAMILY?

"Be fruitful, and multiply and replenish (or fill up) the earth" *(Genesis 1:28)*.

This implies that there was a job to do. Man was to take this planet and cultivate it for divine and human purposes by having families of children.

"And subdue it . . . " *(Genesis 1:28)*.

This implies that there was an enemy to be overcome. Adam and Eve, along with every other couple to follow, had to contend with an enemy, Satan himself.

"And have dominion . . ." *(Genesis 1:28)*

This implies that man was to be Lord of the earth under God, the Lord of the universe.

HOW WAS THE FIRST EARTHLY FAMILY STRUCTURED?

The first earthly family had male headship (I Corinthians 11:3).

Paul the Apostle states that the very fact that man was created first suggests an order of headship *(I Timothy 2:11-15(13); Genesis 2:7, 18, 22).*

Adam began to enter into dominion by naming the animals before the creation of the woman *(Genesis 2:20).*

Eve became a partaker of Adam's name and function. Both of them together were called Man *(Genesis 2:15, 20; 5:2).*

The fact that Adam was the prophet/priest of the family suggests his headship. God had given His command to Adam before He created Eve and, therefore, it was Adam's responsibility to communicate God's law to his wife *(Genesis 2:16, 17, 22; 3:9).*

The fact that God confirmed this order after the fall demonstrates headship *(Genesis 3:16F).* Many feel that male headship in the home was given as a result of the fall, when in reality the fall only necessitated God's explicit statement of the fact. This was a command to the woman that was not necessary to make before the fall because it was fully understood and taken for granted in the order of creation. But now that self-will had been introduced, there was good reason to believe that all human beings would not naturally respond to the authority and the roles that God originally intended for them to fulfill *(Timothy 2:11-15(13); Genesis 20:1-12).*

The first family had plurality of leadership.

The fact that there was something unnatural about the man being alone suggests the need for the woman *(Genesis 2:18, 20).*

The fact that the woman is designated by God as a helper (NAS) indicates her important role in leadership *(Genesis 2:18).* The thought of the word "helper" is "one who is called to the side of, a succourer, an aid". It also means that which is "fitted to, suited to, or appropriate to". The woman is actually the "other part" of the man. She completes him.

The fact that the woman was taken from the side of man seems to confirm that she was to stand alongside him in leadership *(Genesis 2:21).* This suggests that the woman is not created inferior to man, nor was she created to compete with him. The woman was created equal to the man in terms of her person, but distinct from man in terms of her function *(I Corinthians 11:11-12).*

The fact that the man could in no way fulfil the purposes of God without the woman *(Genesis 1:28; 4:1)* demonstrates mutual dependency.

WHAT IS THE SIGNIFICANCE OF THE PROPHECY MADE BY ADAM CONCERNING THE MAN-WOMAN RELATIONSHIP?

"This is now bone of my bones, and flesh of my flesh . . ." (Genesis 2:23) means that man and woman are both made of the same substance. There is an equality of substance, yet again, a distinction of roles.

That common substance was initially dust *(Genesis 2:7).* This indicates that apart from God's grace, we can expect very little from man.

"For this cause a man shall leave his father and his mother . . . " *(Genesis 2:24)* was something that Adam himself never really experienced. He prophesies in regard to future generations. For a man and a woman to fulfill successfully God's purposes, there must be a leaving of parents emotionally and financially.

"And shall cleave to his wife . . ." *(Genesis 2:24)* means to "stick, to adhere, to be glued together, to cling, to hold fast, to remain attached, to be devoted and faithful to something".

"And they shall become one flesh . . ." *(Genesis 2:24)* is one of the greatest miracles that takes place between a man and a woman in harmony with God's plan for their lives. The man and the woman lose their own self-dependence, independence, and self-sufficiency and become one new interdependent being. The miracle of this is prophetical of the relationship of Christ and the Church *(Ephesians 5:28-33).*

SUCH A REALIZATION OF THE IDEAL FIRST EARTHLY FAMILY HELPS US TO UNDERSTAND WHAT CURRENT FACTS THAT DEMONSTRATE JUST THE OPPOSITE?

• The fifty percent divorce rate in America
• The anti-marriage feelings around the world
• The women's liberation movement
• The homosexual revolution
• The unisex concept

• FAMILY PROJECTS •

SECTION 1
LESSON 4
"The First Earthly Family"

"And these words which I command thee this day, shall be in thine heart: And thou shalt teach them diligently unto thy children and shalt talk of them when thou sittest in thine house, and when thou walkest by the way; and when thou liest down, and when thou risest up"
(Deuteronomy 6:6,7).

Project One

☐ Discuss the charge given to the first family in question number two. What does it mean and how does it relate to your family?

DATE ATTEMPTED: _____

RESULTS: _____

_____

_____

Project Two

☐ Discuss what it might have been like had Adam and Eve not sinned. What would the perfect family be like? How does God want your family to change?

DATE ATTEMPTED: _____

RESULTS: _____

_____

_____

Project Three

☐ Discuss the trends of society in question number five and how a biblical understanding of the family would alleviate these problems.

DATE ATTEMPTED: _____

RESULTS: _____

_____

_____

5

The Family As A Miniature Church

SCRIPTURE READING: Ephesians 3:14, 15; 5:1-33

God is a God of order, and He has a plan and a pattern for everything that He does. When God created the human family, not only did it relate to the heavenly family, but it also pointed to the spiritual family of God, the Church. The Bible often refers to the Church as the family of God or the household of faith *(Ephesians 2:19; 3:14, 15; Galatians 6:10)*. To get a better understanding of what the Church should be, we should look at the earthly family, and to get a better understanding of the earthly family, we should examine the function of the Church.

IN WHAT WAYS ARE THE HOME AND THE CHURCH SIMILAR IN STRUCTURE?

Both the home and the church are established on a covenant basis (Genesis 2:24; Ephesians 5:31-32).

Both the home and the church have similar members and similar relationships:

- God the Father *(Matthew 6:9; I Corinthians 11:3)*
- Fathers and mothers *(Mark 10:29-30)*
- An elder brother, the firstborn *(Hebrews 2:14-17; 12:23; Romans 8:29)*
- Many brothers and sisters *(Mark 10:29-30; I Peter 1:22)*

Both the home and the church have a defined membership (Acts 2:41, 47; 5:14; Corinthians 14:23, 26).

Both the home and the church have a plurality of oversight:

- The plural eldership in the local church *(Acts 21:18; I Timothy 5:17, Philippians 1:1)*
- Both the mother and the father in the family *(Matthew 15:4-6; 19:19; Ephesians 6:1-3).*

Both the home and the Church are autonomous social units.

- The self-governing local church *(Revelation 1:4A; 2:1, 8, 12, 18; 3:1, 7, 14)* and the self-governing home *(I Corinthians 11:3; 14:34, 35)*
- The self-supporting local church *(I Corinthians 16:1, 2)* and the self-supporting home *(Proverbs 13:22A; 19:14A; II Corinthians 12:14; I Timothy 5:4)*
- The self-propagating local church *(Acts 2:41, 47; 5:14)* and the self-propagating home *(Genesis 1:28; 4:1; Proverbs 5:15-20)*

IN WHAT WAYS ARE THE HOME AND THE CHURCH SIMILAR IN FUNCTION?

Both the home *(Exodus 12:21-24; Joshua 2:17-21)* and the church *(Isaiah 4:5-6)* provide protection and covering.

Both the home *(Proverbs 29:15)* and the church *(Matthew 18:15-20)* provide a context for discipline.

Both the home *(Deuteronomy 6:7)* and the church *(Matthew 28:19-20)* provide training and instruction.

Both the home and the church are centers for spiritual life.

- Worship in the local church *(I Corinthians 14:15, 26; Ephesians 5:19; Colossians 3:16; Hebrews 13:15)* and in the home *(Hebrews 11:21)*.
- Prayer in the local church *(Luke 19:46, Acts 2:42)* and in the home *(Acts 10:1-4, 30)*
- The Word in the local church *(Acts 2:42)* and in the home *(Deuteronomy 6:4-9)*
- Fellowship in the local church *(Acts 2:42; I John 1:5-7)* and in the home *(Acts 2:46; Ephesians 5:28, 29)*.

Both the home and the church are places of commitment. The members of a family must be committed to each other in:

- Honesty, a willingness to be open and truthful with each other;
- Fellowship, a willingness to spend time with each other;
- Submission, a willingness to respond properly to each other in God-ordained relationships and authority;
- Loyalty, a willingness to use each other's faults as opportunities to support each other;
- Trust and respect, a willingness to give the benefit of the doubt to each other;
- Sobriety, a willingness to take each other seriously;
- Acceptance, a willingness to receive each other just as both of you are.

Both the home *(Exodus 20:12; Psalm 127:3)* and the church *(Psalm 68:5,6; Isaiah 61:3; I Corinthians 12:18, Acts 2:47)* are places where God sovereignly plants people. He does this for the following reasons:

- To develop character in each family member
- To develop ministry in each family member.
- To strengthen the entire family
- To protect each family member from deception and sin
- To fulfill and satisfy each family member
- To begin other solid families eventually

FAMILY • PROJECTS •

SECTION 1
LESSON 5
"The Family As A Miniature Church"

"And these words which I command thee this day, shall be in thine heart: And thou shalt teach them diligently unto thy children and shalt talk of them when thou sittest in thine house, and when thou walkest by the way; and when thou liest down, and when thou risest up"
(Deuteronomy 6:6,7).

Project One ☐ Have a worship service in your family devotional time assigning different parts of the service to each family member. Include some of the following: song leading, special numbers, prayer, testimonies, exhortations. Make it a serious and not too long of a time, however, and expect God to bless everyone.

DATE ATTEMPTED: _____

RESULTS: _____

_____

_____

_____

Project Two ☐ In this lesson we learned that all of the functions in the local church are found in the home in miniature form. Refer to all of the things listed in the lesson and discuss ways in which your family could improve in each area.

DATE ATTEMPTED: _____

RESULTS: _____

_____

_____

_____

6

Loving Leadership

SCRIPTURE READING: Ephesians 5:22-23

WHAT IS LEADERSHIP?

Leadership is the ability to motivate others to follow you to an understood objective.

The word leader itself suggests the existence of a destination or goal. If one is going to lead others, he must have some place in mind to which he is leading them. Jesus underscored the importance of leadership having proper goals when He noted the problems of "the blind leading the blind" (*Matthew 15:14; Luke 6:39*) A leader must have a vision of where he is going, and he must be able to impart that vision to those who follow him. A leader knows what needs to be done, and can persuade others to help him to do it.

A leader of God's people, whether in the church or in the home, must have God-given direction. He must make certain that he is leading his family in the direction that God wants them to go. He must be personally pursuing God's objectives. A leader will not be able to lead his family in a direction that he himself is not going. He must motivate those under him to pursue God's goals, and he must assist them in every way to reach them.

Leadership is the ability to recognize and to develop the potential in others.

A leader must not only be goal-centered. He must also be people-centered. It is not enough for a leader to know where he wants to take his people, he must also be able to see clearly where they are at the present time. If he tries to lead them on a level that they are not on, his desire to help them reach the objectives will be frustrated. Since reaching objectives is a step by step process, a leader must be able to discern what step the people will be able to take next. He must recognize their potential for progress and develop it.

Likewise, a husband and father of a family must recognize the God-given potential in the lives of his family members. He must not try to mold them only into what he wants or needs them to be. But he must help them to become what God wants them to be. He must be more concerned about their developing into what God has called them to be than about accomplishing a certain task. He needs to know those he is leading. The better he knows them, the better he will be able to lead them (*John 2:25*).

WHAT IS THE PURPOSE OF LEADERSHIP?

To provide order in God's creation.

God is a God of order. Beginning with the persons of the Godhead (Father, Son, and Holy Spirit), He has established order *(I Corinthians 15:24; John 16:14a)*. In order for there to be harmony and purpose among any group of things, there must be an orderly arrangement of them in their relatedness to each other. The detailed order throughout God's creation is a witness to the orderliness in God's own nature. Leadership is one of God's ways of maintaining order. God's purpose is that everyone be in submission to others. A father, then, must understand God's order for the home. He must help each family member find their place in that order and properly respond to it.

To provide channels of God's authority over creation.

When God created man, He declared that one of His purposes was to share His function of authority and dominion over creation *(Genesis 1:26-28)*. God decided to delegate His own authority to others so that His rule could be extended and administered throughout creation. This choice was made not out of necessity, but out of God's desire to share His entire being with man. Thus, leadership involved authority. The purpose of leadership is to be a channel for God's authority. Those who try to lead apart from God's authority, will not be able to bring others into the fulfillment of God's purposes for them.

So, a father must recognize that he is to be a leader with authority. He is not to exercise a self-assumed authority but must become a channel for God's authority by his own personal submission to it. The family will have difficulty submitting to a father that is not in submission to the authority over him.

WHAT IS GOD'S ORDER OF LEADERSHIP IN THE HOME?

Plural Oversight.

The Scripture declares that "two are better than one" *(Ecclesiastes 4:9)*. This is especially true when it comes to guiding the affairs of the home. Plural leadership is taught throughout Scripture in relation to every level of government. Multiple counsel is strongly encouraged in Proverbs 11:14; 15:22 and 24:6. In keeping with His ways and the plurality of counsel in His own triune being, God has ordained that there be plural leadership in the home. This, according to Scripture, should normally consist of a husband and a wife, a father and a mother *(Genesis 2:24; 28:7; Exodus 20:12; Proverbs 1:8; 10:1; 23:22,24,25)*.

Chain of Command.

Although God's way of leadership includes plural oversight, there is to be an order of headship within that plurality. Although the husband and wife stand co-equal in the sight of God "being heirs together of the grace of life" *(I Peter 3:7)*, the man is chosen by God to bear the responsibility of being the head of the home. The husband is called to submit to God, the wife is called to submit to her husband, and the children are called to submit to their parents. Although all the members of the family are equally valuable to God, and equally important for the success of the home, God has established this chain of command for the sake of effective leadership in the home *(I Corinthians 11:3; Ephesians 5:22-24; 6:1-4)*.

THE FAMILY'S VALUE & IMPORTANCE BEFORE GOD.

THE FAMILY'S ORDER & ROLE BEFORE GOD.

WHAT MAKES LEADERSHIP EFFECTIVE?

Provision:

In the work that Christ has done for us, He is both our provision and our example. He is not only the example of what we are to become, but He provides us with the help and motivation that we need to succeed. When He laid down His life for us in love, He provided us with all we need to accomplish God's purpose for us. His sacrificial love is our provision and the basis for our motivation to follow His leadership. It is to be the same in the home. Although the husband is the head of the wife, it is to be his sacrificial love for her that motivates her to submit to his leadership. Children also thrive on loving concern *(I Thessalonians 2:7,8.11)*. The following qualities will motivate family members to respond to the father's leadership in the home: sacrificial love, selfless commitment, personal concern, faithfulness, loyalty, gentleness, patience, mercy, forgiveness, openness, and availability.

Example:

Christ also motivated people to follow Him by His example *(John 13:14,15)*. He requires this of those who lead His people *(I Peter 5:3)*. A husband, too, must be an example to his wife, and they together must be examples to their children. They must model the character and lifestyle that they desire their children to imitate. Proclaiming a standard which they do not follow themselves will only frustrate and drain the motivation out of their children to reach that standard. The father and then the mother should each be an example of the following qualities: faithfulness, promptness, responsibility, obedience, attentiveness, contentment, neatness, diligence, joyfulness, hospitality, and gratefulness.

WHAT IS LOVING LEADERSHIP?

Loving leadership is God's way of leadership. It is motivated by a godly concern for others rather than self-seeking desires. Doing what is best for others is never as easy as pleasing oneself. It takes more strength to love others into submitting to God's will than to force them into surrendering to your will. The nature of loving leadership can be revealed by contrasting it with domineering leadership.

LOVING LEADERSHIP:	DOMINEERING LEADERSHIP:
• Leads towards God's goals	• Leads towards self-centered or manipulative goals
• Has others' best interests in mind	• Has own best interests in mind
• Provides an example to follow	• Expects conformity without a model
• Recognizes others' limitations	• Drives others beyond their limitations
• Demonstrates personal concern	• Takes people for granted
• Shows sacrificial love	• Takes advantage of people
• Releases others' potentials	• Stifles others' development
• Is a humble channel for God's authority	• Proclaims self-assumed authority
• Remains open to correction	• Is not ajustable
• Values others' opinions	• Ignores others' opinions
• Evidences a humble spirit	• Evidences an air of superiority
• Demonstrates a servant's heart	• Expects others always to serve him
• Gives credit where credit is due	• Takes credit for others' accomplishments
• Brings others to maturity	• Makes others increasingly dependent on him
• Uses discipline to help and to instruct others	• Uses discipline to punish and to revenge others

Although some aspects of domineering leadership may sometimes produce some results, they will tend to be superficial and short-lived. Only loving leadership will produce the quality of results that will last for eternity.

We should periodically take time to evaluate our leadership, pinpoint areas in which we are weak, and take definite steps of action to change them.

• FAMILY PROJECTS •

SECTION 1
LESSON 6
"Loving Leadership"

"And these words which I command thee this day, shall be in thine heart: And thou shalt teach them diligently unto thy children and shalt talk of them when thou sittest in thine house, and when thou walkest by the way; and when thou liest down, and when thou risest up"
(Deuteronomy 6:6,7).

Project One ☐ The father should share with each member of the family, including his wife, the potential he sees in them, and the goals he feels God has for them. This could lead to a discussion of how these things can be accomplished. This may require previous careful preparation. Single parents should also do this.

DATE ATTEMPTED: _____

RESULTS: _____

_____

Project Two ☐ Draw a picture of your family's chain of command, complete with names, and discuss how each one can help improve the way that it functions. Be specific and sincere. Plan a time when you will evaluate your progress together.

DATE ATTEMPTED: _____

RESULTS: _____

_____

Project Three ☐ Let the husband/father and wife/mother evaluate their leadership using the qualities listed under Question 4, and the contrasts under Question 5. This can be done alone, together, or with the entire family giving input. Steps should be taken to work on at least one of the weak areas discovered.

DATE ATTEMPTED: _____

RESULTS: _____

_____

7

Effective Submission

SCRIPTURE READING: Ephesians 5:22-33; I Peter 3; Hebrews 13:17

WHAT IS SUBMISSION?

Submission is to yield to the authority of another; to surrender to defer to the judgment or the discretion of another; to comply with; to be subject to *(Websters Dictionary)*.

Submission is to yield the option of leading in order to follow. Any person can exercise their option of leading in any given situation. Submission is yielding that option of leading to another and choosing to follow for the sake of order and/or unity. In a marriage, both husband and wife are capable of leading, but for both to lead simultaneously would mean chaos and confusion. Thus, someone must give up their option of leading.

Submission is also the ability to bring out the best in others by yielding to their commands, opinions, or suggestions *(I Peter 3:1-b)*. As a wife submits to the leadership of her husband, she enters into her God-ordained role in the relationship. In doing so, she releases the grace of God in her husband's life for him to become the best man, husband, and father that he can possibly be *(I Peter 3:1, 7)*.

WHAT IS THE PURPOSE OF SUBMISSION?

Submission demonstrates God's own nature and being to the world.

Scripture makes it very clear to us that God is a God of order *(I Corinthians 14:33, 40)*. He has created an order in all things that exist just like He has an order in his own very being in the triune Godhead. The Holy Spirit submits to the Son *(John 16:14A)*. The Son submits to the Father *(I Corinthians 15:24)*.

Submission ensuris a successful home.

A husband and a wife must understand and practice the concept of submission in God's order for the home. For each partner to take their divinely appointed role, is to produce an order and a stability that will contribute to a smooth running home. Failing to implement God's order for submission in the home creates a disorder that will cancel out much good in the home. This failure will eventually destroy the home's effectiveness in the world, in the church, and in the lives of the family members.

Submission teaches God-ordained roles to the children.

God has designed an order for the home by specifically naming the roles that each member is to take. These roles constitute basically two kinds: leading and following. The Word of God specifically names who in the marriage takes which role *(I Corinthians 11:3)*. God in His sovereign wisdom, even designed the very nature of the man and the very nature of the woman in accordance with this order *(Genesis 3:16; I Timothy 2:9-15; I Peter 3:1-7, Titus 2:5)*. As the husband takes the initiative and the responsibility that comes with the leadership role, and as the wife assumes the role of responder and follower, divine order is established. This divine order serves as a basic foundation for all of the relationships in the home. If these roles are confused or reversed by husband and wife, the children grow up with distorted concepts of what their roles in life are to be. This order requires a submission on the part of every member. Let the following diagram serve to illustrate:

Submission makes a home available for God's blessing.

As the woman submits to her husband, and the husband submits to Christ, the same order is established on earth that is in heaven in the Godhead. As the wife obeys, submits to, and reverences her husband, she takes her part in the structure of the home to set up the conditions for blessing, health, and fulfillment for all the other members of the home as well as for herself. Notice in the diagram that as a woman submits to her husband, she is submitting to God *(Ephesians 5:22)*. If a wife does not submit to her own hsuband, she takes herself out of divine order, and thus is not in a position to submit to God. In fact, she is not in submission to God. The only time a woman could rightfully violate this order, is if her husband required her to take an action that would diametrically oppose an essential biblical truth. This kind of action should only be taken with serious prayer, thought, wisdom, and counsel.

Even during these kind of times, a wife must keep a submissive *attitude* all the while. For example, the Apostles did not obey the city rulers, yet they submitted to the consequences of their disobedience with a submissive attitude *(Acts 16:19-34)*.

WHAT DO WE MEAN BY EFFECTIVE SUBMISSION?

Effective submission is a genuine display of the earnest and humble response of the wife to the leadership of the husband that results in God's blessing. A submissive lifestyle releases the grace of God in a greater way into the husband and wife relationship. Furthermore, it sets up the creative potential for bringing every family member into their highest level of spiritual and natural achievement.

Effective submission brings a greater amount of God's grace into the husband-wife relationship.

Scripture tells us that husband and wife heirs *together* of the grace (divine enablement) of God *(I Peter 3:7)*. As the wife submits to her husband, and the husband honors his wife, so the grace of God flows into the relationship to the extent of having prayers answered *(I Peter 3:1-7)*. Since a relationship is the result of what two people mutually contribute to it, it is logical that if either party fails to contribute spiritually the relationship suffers. When the wife is submitting to her husband, she introduces into her relationship with her husband the omnipotent grace of God. This is such a powerful, redemptive force that God's Word says that by this indirect means she releases God to bring about dramatic change in him *(I Peter 3:1-6)*. What a tremendous privilege! This dynamic truth of submission challenges the husband to take his leadership role, makes it easier for him to do so, and establishes an important foundation for God's dealings in her life and his. Her husband now has only God with whom to contend. He cannot use her lack of submission as an excuse not to submit to God. Facing God alone *(I Corinthians 11:3)*, the husband is sure to change.

Effective submission produces the creative potential for bringing every family member into his or her highest level of spiritual and natural achievement.

Scripture tells us that God gives grace to the humble *(James 4:6)*. It naturally follows that according to the degree of humility, so is the degree of grace granted. As the wife humbly submits herself to her husband in every area of their life together, she receives God's grace to be her best. When she is at her best emotionally, spiritually, mentally, physically, and socially she is then in a position truly to aid her husband and the children in being their best in natural and spiritual areas. There is no greater witness of God in the home, than a wife who is responsive to her husband, a positive encouragement to her children, and a selfless servant of others in the church and in the community.

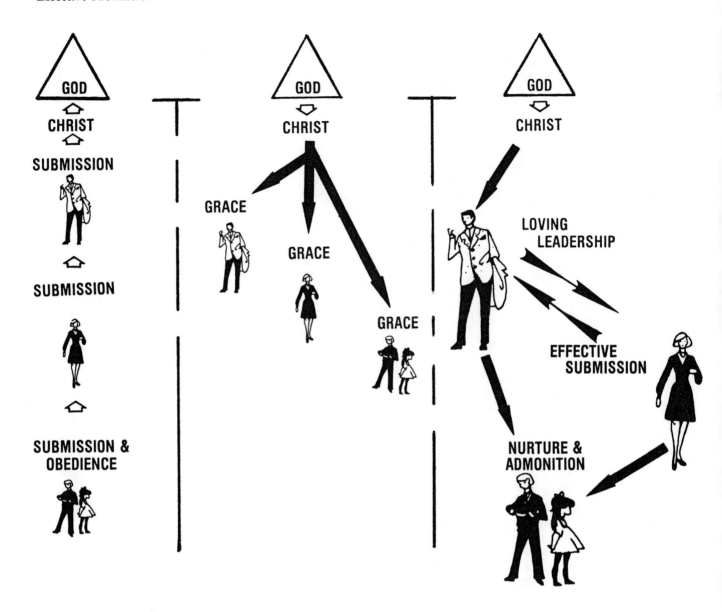

WHAT DOES EFFECTIVE SUBMISSION REQUIRE?

Successful submission requires faith. Submission on the part of the wife requires that she recognize that this route is God's will even if it is contrary to her own feelings *(I Peter 3:5, 6)*. This does not mean that a wife is responsible to share her opinion only when it agrees with her husband's *(Matthew 27:17-19)*. She must trust that God will use her submission for good *(Romans 8:28)* even though it might mean that her husband make a poor decision. This is all part of successful submission.

Effective submission requires humility. Scripture likens the relationship between Christ and the Church to the husband and wife relationship *(Ephesians 5:23-33)*. In this analogy, the role of Christ to the Church is seen in three distinct areas:

- Christ is the Head of the Church;
- Christ is the Savior of the Body; and
- Christ is Lord of every believer.

These three aspects give us a view of how the wife is to view her husband.

- First, the wife must see her husband as her head *(Ephesians 5:23)*. She recognizes his authority and places herself under it.

- Secondly, the wife realizes that her husband is to be her *savior (Ephesians 5:23, 28, 29)*. He is to be her protector, deliverer, and preserver. By submitting to him, she allows him to take this role.

- Thirdly, the wife must see her husband as her *lord (I Peter 3:6)*. She does not see him as *the Lord,* but as an earthly representative of the Lord Jesus Christ.

Therefore, the wife can approach her husband with a great reverence and respect without hypocrisy and insincerity even as Sarah of old. This inward heart-reflection of "esteem, of placing up on a high place, and of godly reverence" will go a long way towards making him the man that God wants him to be. He, at the outset of marriage, might be a rather poor earthly representative of Jesus Christ, but a submission to him will go much further in bringing about growth and change than nagging, harrassment, and constant criticism. It is only as she places him in this position that he will achieve God's best in his role in the home. Sarah suffered from some of Abraham's blunders, but her attitude toward him eventually made him "the father of all who believe". This humility, which is placing one's self lower than others *(Philippians 2:3-7),* is an essential ingredient to effective submission. It is this heart attitude that makes submission possible, especially under trying circumstances. The wife can count on God's enabling strength to be able to do this *(James 4:6, 7).*

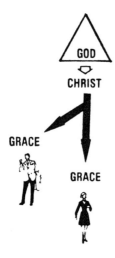

Successful submission also requires sincerity. Some wives externally submit to their husbands only to get something out of them. This is a sinful attitude. A wife must submit internally and sincerely. The following chart compares sincere successful submission with insincere token submission.

EFFECTIVE SUBMISSION:	**TOKEN SUBMISSION:**
• Seeks others' best interest	• Seeks self-interest
• Acknowledges authority	• Resents authority
• Promotes ideas of others	• Seeks to validate own opinions
• Desires to please	• Seeks to be pleased
• Complies both internally and externally	• Complies externally only
• Receives and responds to correction	• Resists adjustment and correction
• Serves others wholeheartedly	• Serves others half-heartedly
• Looks for direction	• Evades direction

By token submission, the wife may be able to manipulate her husband, but it will bring her into the bondage of her own self-centered desires. True submission liberates the wife to find true fulfillment in life.

FAMILY PROJECTS

● F A M I L Y   P R O J E C T S ●

SECTION 2
LESSON 7
"Successful Submission"

"And these words which I command thee this day, shall be in thine heart: And thou shalt teach them diligently unto thy children and shalt talk of them when thou sittest in thine house, and when thou walkest by the way; and when thou liest down, and when thou risest up"
(Deuteronomy 6:6,7).

Project One ☐

Discuss the meaning of submission. Have each family member give his own definition. Use appropriate analogies to illustrate submission, eg. policeman and traffic, teacher and students, etc.

DATE ATTEMPTED: _____

RESULTS: _____

_____

_____

Project Two ☐

Have a private discussion between husband and wife, on what makes submission to his leadership difficult at times. Focus on any wrong attitudes that need to be changed on either part.

DATE ATTEMPTED: _____

RESULTS: _____

_____

_____

Project Three ☐

Discuss with each family member ways in which they can bring about greater harmony in the home through practical expressions of submission.

DATE ATTEMPTED: _____

RESULTS: _____

_____

_____

8

Maintaining Covenant Relationship

SCRIPTURE READING: I Corinthians 13

The marriage contract is the establishment of a covenant between two people. God Himself has set the pattern for all covenants in His relationship to man. God's covenant with man is often interpreted as a marriage covenant *(Ezekiel 16:8,60)*. When God entered into His covenant with man, His covenant was based on certain character qualities within Himself that made such a covenant possible. If we want our relationships to be successful, we must look to the highest source for our pattern, and learn all we can from God's relationship to us.

WHAT IS THE DEFINITION OF A "COVENANT"?

A covenant is a "formal, solemn, and binding agreement made between two or more parties".

The O.T. word for "covenant" comes from a word meaning "bond" and literally means "to bind two (or more) parties together".

WHAT IS THE NATURE OF THE COVENANT THAT GOD MADE WITH MAN?

The covenants that God made with man were of a very serious nature. God even instructs man never to take vows lightly *(Ecclesiastes 5:45)*. Therefore, when God Himself makes a covenant, He has no intention of breaking it. He intends for it to be everlasting *(Genesis 9:14-16; Judges 2:1)*.

WHAT QUALITIES DOES GOD MANIFEST IN ENTERING INTO AND MAINTAINING A COVENANT RELATIONSHIP WITH MAN?

The love of God (Deuteronomy 7:6-8).

God is never motivated by self-interest or selfishness, but He chose to enter into covenant relationship because of His divine love.

The faithfulness of God (Deuteronomy 7:9).

God is absolutely faithful because He is stable and unchanging in His commitments. He is a rock, and we can depend on the fact that if He made a vow today, it will be still in His heart to keep that vow tomorrow *(Hebrews 6:16-20)*.

The forgiveness of God (Psalm 130:4).

God maintains His faithfulness to the covenant because He readily forgives the offenses of repentant men.

The selflessness of God (Philippians 2:3-8).

God loved the world so much that He sacrifically gave of Himself to establish a covenant relationship *(John 3:16).*

IN WHAT WAY DO THESE QUALITIES IN GOD FORM THE BASIS FOR A SUCCESSFUL MARRIAGE COVENANT?

The love of God must be the base of every marriage covenant (I Corinthians 13).

A man and a woman need more than physical attraction. They need a divine love between them that is not based on external circumstances. This love can only come from God *(Ephesians 5:25; Colossians 3:14; I Thessalonians 3:11-13; 4:9-12).*

Faithfulness to each other must be purposed by both covenanted marriage partners.

If there is ever any hint by either party that the marriage relationship is anything less than permanent, a time of crisis will bring certain failure. Just as God's faithfulness extends to all facets of His relationship to man *(I Thessalonians 5:24; II Thessalonians 3:3; Hebrews 10:23-25; 11:11-12),* so should marital faithfulness *(cf. Psalm 12:1; Proverbs 20:6; Isaiah 1:26).*

Forgiveness must be an operating principle in a successful marriage covenant.

• Forgiveness means "to release from debt". It involves a "putting aside, a disregarding, a putting away completely and unreservedly" the sins of another *(Romans 3:25).*

• True forgiveness involves a determination never to bring the subject of offense up again *(Isaiah 38:17; Micah 7:18,19; Jeremiah 31:31-34; Psalm 103:3, 8-12).*

• Forgiveness is part of the duty of the Christian *(Matthew 18:21-35).*

• An unforgiving spirit is a sin greater than the original offense in God's mind *(Matthew 18:34-35).*

• If we fail to forgive, we will live in torment *(Matthew 18:34,35).*

• God's forgiveness toward us *(Colossians 1:14)* is dependent upon our forgiveness of others *(Matthew 5:23,24; 6:12; Mark 11:25; Luke 6:36,37; Colossians 3:13).*

Selflessness must be in the heart of each marriage covenant partner.

Unless both members of a marriage are putting the interest of the other before themselves *(Romans 12:10; Philippians 2:3,4),* there is bound to be tension, jealousy, impatience, stubborness, argumentativeness, criticism, harshness, pride and oversensitivity. For true harmony to exist, there must be a death to self and an exaltation of Christ *(Mark 8:34-38).*

There are many traits in each of us that reflect the attitude of selfishness or living for ourselves. Check any of the following areas in which you may manifest selfishness:

☐ A spirit of exaltation and pride, feeling that you are better than the others

☐ A love of human praise, a seeking to be noticed

☐ A centering of conversation around yourself and your own interests

☐ A spirit of impatience with others

☐ A spirit of retaliation or resentment when opposed or contradicted

☐ A tendency to criticize and pick flaws when others have been successful

☐ A tendency to rebuke through sarcastic expressions

☐ A jealous disposition and a secret spirit of envy

Because the qualities of love, faithfulness, forgiveness, and selflessness abound in God, God is able to keep covenant with His people in spite of their many failings. These qualities must abound in us if we are to maintain the covenant that we established with our spouse.

• FAMILY PROJECTS •

SECTION 2
LESSON 8
"Maintaining Covenant Relationship"

"And these words which I command thee this day, shall be in thine heart: And thou shalt teach them diligently unto thy children and shalt talk of them when thou sittest in thine house, and when thou walkest by the way; and when thou liest down, and when thou risest up"
(Deuteronomy 6:6,7).

Project One ☐ Have each member of the family read *I Corinthians 13:4-8a,* putting their own name in wherever the word "charity" or "love" occurs. Have them write down their greatest area of strength and their greatest area of weakness. Discuss your answer among the other members of the family. Have the smaller children list or draw ways that they can show love to other family members. Encourage them to be as specific as possible.

DATE ATTEMPTED: _____

RESULTS: _____

_____

_____

_____

_____

Project Two ☐ Have each member of the family write down or share with you specific ways that they can be less selfish in their relationship to other members of the family. Discuss each answer, giving encouragement to each other in setting positive goals to overcome selfishness.

DATE ATTEMPTED: _____

RESULTS: _____

_____

_____

_____

9

Communicating in a Marriage

SCRIPTURE READING: Ephesians 4:29-32

WHY IS COMMUNICATION IN MARRIAGE IMPORTANT?

In order for two people to relate to each other with meaning and harmony there must be communication *(Amos 3:3)*. Since two very different persons are involved in a marriage, there will be differing opinions, views, sets of values, desires, and methods. It therefore becomes vitally necessary for communication to occur regularly. Since marriage is a "covenant of companionship" *(Genesis 2:18),* and the goal is to become one in judgment, decision and action, a great deal of "agreeing" must take place. This can only come about through effective communication.

WHAT IS COMMUNICATION?

Communication is the act or instance of transmitting a verbal or written message. It is a process by which information is exchanged between individuals through a common system of symbols, signs, or behavior. It is simply the exchange of information *(Webster's Dictionary).*

WHAT IN MAN OR WOMAN AFFECTS ONE'S COMMUNICATING ABILITY?

Character is the steering mechanism of communication. According to one's character, so will one communicate. If one is self-centered, his communication will be so. If one is selfless, his communication will also reflect the same *(Matthew 12:34).*

Sin polluted man's ability to communicate in a positive, unifying way. Because sin introduced selfishness into man's character, only the cross of Christ through salvation can restore the ability to communicate effectively and harmoniously.

The following are some of the results of sin upon man's communicating ability:

- A desire not to communicate *(Genesis 3:8)*
- A tendency to shift blame for failures *(Genesis 3:12,13)*
- A tendency to lie and be deceitful *(Genesis 4:9)*
- A tendency to conceal oneself from one's mate *(Genesis 3:7)*

Since the intimacy and openness that Adam and Eve enjoyed in *Genesis 2:25* was broken by sin, they naturally were inclined to conceal themselves from one another *(Genesis 3:7)*. Before sin, there was nothing hidden between themselves and God and nothing hidden between each other, but sin destroyed that. Because sin built walls between man and woman, the more sinless each mate becomes, the more their ability to communicate in a unifying way increases. Since a relationship is "that which exists between two persons as a result of their individual contribution", it logically follows that whatever goes into the relationship will make up the relationship. If anger, resentment, bitterness, selfishness, and fear are contributed to the relationship through certain attitudes, actions, and conversations, the relationship will be anemic. If the input from both husband and wife is love, trust, consideration, and kindness, the relationship will be a blessing and a source of joy to both. The following diagram illustrates the choice that each marriage partner has in what they contribute to their marriage relationship.

RELATIONSHIP

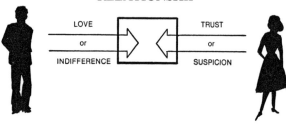

IS COMMUNICATION ITSELF ALWAYS A POSITIVE, CONSTRUCTIVE THING?

No. There are two kinds of communication: unifying and divisive. *Ephesians 4:29* makes this very clear. All communication will either tend to build up or to destroy the relationship. God wants marriage partners to speak the truth, but to speak it in love *(Ephesians 4:15)*.

WHAT THEN ARE THE KEYS TO COMMUNICATING HARMONIOUSLY IN MARRIAGE?

Two important keys to harmonious communication are: quantity of communication and quality of communication. We can see both of these in the pattern relationship for all human relationships: the vertical relationship that God desires to have with us. The principles that we see in our relationship to Christ are the same ones that should govern our relationship to our spouse *(Ephesians 5:22-25, 32)*.

• Scripture speaks of a *quantity* of communication that God expects us to have with Him *(Hebrews 13:15; I Thessalonians 5:17; Ephesians 6:18; Psalm 34:1)*. The phrases "at all times", "continually", and "always", underscore the fact that a *quantity* of constant communication is necessary to develop and maintain our relationship with God. It is also vitally necessary to have a *quantity* of constant communication in marriage. With the countless number of issues, problems, and choices that are daily confronted in marriage, it is easy to see that a sizeable amount of communication is necessary in order to "walk together" *(Amos 3:3)*.

• Scripture speaks of a *quality* of communication necessary to develop and maintain a relationship *(Ephesians 4:29-31; I Peter 3:8-10)*. What a tremendous challenge: never to speak anything to your mate that is not edifying. It is very easy to find the negatives that are common to every home beginning to eclipse all of the positives through divisive and explosive conversation. Regardless of who was initially responsible for the first inflammatory word, both are immediately held responsible before God to forgive and to re-establish their love relationship as the basis for their communication *(James 5:16, Ephesians 4:32)*. Words are powerful to bless or to belittle. Make a valiant effort to be positive about negative things. Negative situations must be discussed at times, but they can be discussed in a positive vein, with a faith-view to their solution.

WHAT ARE SOME PRACTICAL SUGGESTIONS FOR DEALING WITH COMMUNICATION BREAKDOWN?

DO'S

• Ask for forgiveness for wrong attitudes and abusive language *(Ephesians 4:32)*.

• Set prearranged times for discussion of subjects that are sensitive or potentially explosive.

• Pray together before discussing "hot" items *(Ephesians 4:3)*.

• In humility, ask your spouse how you can improve your communication, as well as what adjustments they would like you to make in each specific issue.

• If through prayer and diligent effort you are unable to solve essential issues, seek qualified counsel.

DON'TS

• Don't attach your spouse's character or personality *(Galatians 5:15)*.

• Don't raise issues again that have already been settled just becaue they didn't turn out in your favor.

• Don't attempt to make or force your spouse to conform to your point of view, but don't fail to give them the opportunity to agree with you.

• Don't be against a compromise. Sometimes the best or only solution lies in a portion of each view.

• Don't be unwilling to sacrifice your view for the good of the relationship and the best interest of your mate.

FAMILY • PROJECTS •

SECTION 2
LESSON 9

"Communicating in a Marriage"

"And these words which I command thee this day, shall be in thine heart: And thou shalt teach them diligently unto thy children and shalt talk of them when thou sittest in thine house, and when thou walkest by the way; and when thou liest down, and when thou risest up"
(Deuteronomy 6:6,7).

Project One

☐ This week set aside a time which you and your spouse can ask each other:

- Do I communicate enough (quantity)? If not, how can *we* work together on this?
- How can we improve the quality of our communication? Do we pray together?

DATE ATTEMPTED: _____

RESULTS: _____

_____

_____

Project Two

☐ Ask your wife/husband for a pre-arranged time to talk about three issues that need discussion (e.g. spiritual atmosphere of home, use of television, spiritual development of children, present financial state, etc.). Remember to keep in mind the principles that we have discussed in this lesson.

DATE ATTEMPTED: _____

RESULTS: _____

_____

_____

Project Three

☐ Agree on how we should handle our disagreements in the future, e.g. not name-calling, not crying, not yelling, not leaving, not refusing to talk, not bringing up forgiven offenses, etc.

DATE ATTEMPTED: _____

RESULTS: _____

_____

_____

Resolving Marital Irritations

SCRIPTURE READING: I Peter 3:9-11; Romans 12:18; Matthew 5:9

WHAT IS AN IRRITATION?

An irritation is "an incident, conversation, or situation that has the ability to exasperate, nettle, provoke, rile, peeve, or anger a person or persons".

WHY DOES MARRIAGE HAVE THE UNIQUE POTENTIAL FOR IRRITATIONS?

Marriage has the unique potential for irritations because it is the coming together of two persons into oneness. In order for oneness to occur, there must be the merging of two differing personalities, backgrounds, perspectives, and lifestyles. Because of this "differentness" there is the potential for irritations. Whenever two people choose to come together in marital intimacy, there arises the need for coordination of efforts, plans, and decisions. This process of making two lifestyles into one gives rise to possible irritations in the following areas:

Matters of Personal Habit:

• How one squeezes the toothpaste
• How one puts things away or doesn't put things away
• How one dresses
• Personal hygiene
• Driving technique
• Nylons adorning the bathroom
• Cold feet in bed
• The newspaper "wall"
• The T.V. drone

Matters of Differing Taste:

• Whether to buy this color or that color, this brand or that brand

• This route to a location or that route

• This kind of furnishing or that kind

• Whether to do what he wants tonight or what she wants

Matters of Social Habit:

- Corny or unfunny jokes
- Monopolizing conversation
- Just watching everybody else talk
- Interrupting constantly
- Adjusting poor memories of past events
- Being picky about unessential details

Matters of Household Management:

- Writing checks but not recording them in register
- Waiting to clean the living room until company comes
- Unequal treatment of the children
- Eternal minor household repairs
- Not washing out the bathtub
- Windows open or closed at night
- The electric blanket's temperature setting

In all of the aforementioned areas, there are opportunities for differing points of view which could give rise to irritations. Irritations can give rise to conflicts. These matters are a part of every day living together that must be solved and worked out in order to maintain the peace of God in the home.

ARE THESE TIMES WHEN ONE IS MORE SUSCEPTIBLE TO BEING IRRITATED? IF SO, WHEN ARE THOSE TIMES?

The following times are times when people are more subject to being irritated:

- When one is tired;
- When one is hungry;
- When one is in a hurry;
- When one is sick;
- When one is depressed or angry;
- During hormonal changes (menstrual cycles and "change of life");
- When one is fasting;
- Any combination of the above.

During these times one should take extra precaution to be more sensitive, tolerant, understanding, and patient. These are times when one is not at his/her best. To be aware of these conditions and to respond in a Christ-like manner is to strengthen the marriage relationship. Timing is a factor that must be recognized *(Ecclesiastes 3:1-8)*.

During these times, one should avoid things that would cause irritation. For example, avoid:

- Bringing up today's negative events;

- Opening up an issue that requires a policy-decision for the future, and which will require more time to discuss and conclude than is allowable at that time;
- Making even constructive criticism of bad habits;
- Looking with a critical eye at the meal that is served;
- Making big things out of little things;
- Verbally noticing things that are undone.

WHAT BIBLICAL ATTITUDES HELP TO OVERCOME MARITAL IRRITATIONS?

The Attitude of a Peacemaker:

Scripture says that happiness and blessing are the rewards of a peacemaker *(Matthew 5:9)*. Both husband and wife should make a constant effort to preserve and maintain peace between themselves *(Romans 12:18; I Peter 3:9-11)*. This will necessitate sensitivity, humility, and a forgiving heart.

Both the husband and the wife must value marital peace as more important than insisting on their own individual ways.

The Attitude of Submission:

There must be a giving attitude on the part of both husband and wife *(Ephesians 5:21)*. The success and happiness of a marriage is somewhat dependent upon the degree of willingness to defer to the desire or taste of one's mate. Choosing to honor and concede to your spouse's desire or choice will eliminate many irritations and immediately produce unity *(Romans 12:10)*.

The Attitude of Forbearance:

A disposition of tolerance, patience, and long-suffering is vitally necessary to stave off irritation-producing situations. In order not to be overcome by evil, but to overcome evil with good *(Romans 12:21)*, each must take his/her responsibility to:

- Hold their tongue when necessary;
- Speak softly and tactfully;
- Ask for forgiveness after an offense;
- Have a proper sense of timing to what one says and does.

The enduring nature of forbearance will make this possible.

The Attitude of Love:

Love for one's mate will seek the benefit, comfort, and convenience of him/her *(I Corinthians 13:5)*. Love will endure until a solution has been achieved *(I Corinthians 13:7, 8)*.

True divine love for each other will not keep a record of past irritations or wrongs *(I Corinthians 13:5)*.

The Attitude of Meekness:

This is the attitude that both husband and wife must have to insure harmony in marriage. Meekness is yielding one's rights and expectations to God rather than insisting on them. To make an idol of what ''I want changed in you'', will only breed resentment and competition. Only God can ultimately change one's mate for lasting good and bring him/her to a place where he/she meets my needs *(Psalm 62:5).*

WHAT PRACTICAL STEPS SHOULD BE TAKEN TO AVOID AND REMOVE IRRITATIONS?

• In your own private prayer time, yield your rights and expectations to God.

• Take note of how you are saying what you are saying. How would you yourself respond to what you are saying if it was being said to you?

• Take note of your timing. As yourself, ''is this the proper time to bring this up?''

• Ask forgiveness if you offend your mate in word or action.

• Be willing to compromise.

• Be willing to do something your spouse's way, if compromise does not appear appropriate or forthcoming.

• Take note of your tone of voice.

CHECK THE LOVE-LEVEL OF YOUR MARRIAGE

	YES	NO
Do I really hear the criticisms and adjustments that my spouse suggests?	☐	☐
Am I making an effort to please him/her by willingly making those adjustments?	☐	☐
Have I allowed my irritations over things that my spouse does to eclipse my love and appreciation for him/her?	☐	☐
Do I express my appreciation for the small things that are done for me?	☐	☐

• FAMILY PROJECTS •

SECTION 2
LESSON 10
"Intermittent Irritations"

"And these words which I command thee this day, shall be in thine heart: And thou shalt teach them diligently unto thy children and shalt talk of them when thou sittest in thine house, and when thou walkest by the way; and when thou liest down, and when thou risest up"
(Deuteronomy 6:6,7).

Project One ☐ Discuss with your spouse what your irritations with each other are. Work through them to solutions and resolutions on as many as possible (limit of 3). Mutually surrender to God in prayer those that don't seem to work out.

DATE ATTEMPTED: _____

RESULTS: _____

_____

_____

_____

Project Two ☐ Discuss with the whole family some of the irritations of other family members. Have each member write out one irritation that he/she has with each other member. Include with the irritation what they believe the solution is. Ask the smaller children to verbalize their concerns.

DATE ATTEMPTED: _____

RESULTS: _____

_____

_____

_____

11

Sex in Marriage

SCRIPTURE READING: Song of Solomon 1-2

WHAT IS THE CHRISTIAN VIEW OF SEX?

As with all other areas of life, Christians must accept God's view of sex.

• First, we must recognize that sex was God's idea. Its origin in God's mind invites us to be optimistic about its place in our lives. It was created by God for good and not evil. It is a good gift intended by God to produce great joy and not sorrow.

• Second, the God-intended benefits of sex can only be experienced as we use it in harmony with His purpose. Marriage is the only context God sanctions for sexual expression because sex was meant to set marriage apart from all other relationships. Though other aspects of marriage can be shared with other people (eating, conversing, friendship, etc.) sex cannot because it signifies the kind of unique life-commitment that constitutes a marriage!

• Third, the worldly abuse of sex should not be allowed to destroy our confidence in its positive value. In opposing the negatives of the world's view of sex,

many Christians have ignored the positives of God's view. They have used the Bible's prohibitions to fight the abuse of sex without realizing that an understanding of God's positive purpose for sex is what makes the prohibitions effective *(Proverbs 6:32)*. This has produced an unhealthy negative attitude toward sex. Christians should be as much *for* the right use of sex as they are *opposed* to its abuse.

• Fourth, the privacy and sanctity of sex in marriage must be upheld. Sex is sacred because it is to be a reflection of the union possible between God and man *(Ephesians 5:31, 32; I Corinthians 6:16, 17)*, represents the total intimacy of the marriage relationship *(Genesis 2:23-25)*, and it is the means by which new lives are brought into existence *(Genesis 4:1)*. Thus, sex is to be a secret and private thing, not because it is evil or shameful but because it is holy and meaningful.

Hebrews 13:4 summarizes the Christian view of sex: "Marriage is honourable in all, and the bed undefiled: but whoremongers and adulterers God will judge".

• "Marriage is honourable" means the marriage is to be esteemed as 'the highest form of human relationship modelling godly virtues'.

- "The bed undefiled" means that, in the confines of marriage the bed is a clean and holy place of special delight, refreshment, comfort, strength, invigoration, communion, and nurture.

- "But whoremongers and adulterers" means that it is possible to abuse and misuse the God-given joy of sex. The marriage bed must be kept undefiled, that is, guarded and preserved from all unfaithfulness and selfish exploitation.

- "God will judge" means that marital sex is such an important issue that God will not allow misuse to go unchecked.

WHAT PLACE DOES SEX HAVE IN LIFE?

It is a Part of Life

Sex must be viewed as having a small place in life, as being non-essential without being non-existent. It is when sex is not kept in its proper place that many problems arise. The following statements and illustrations will serve to give this perspective.

- Life is more than marriage.
  Our walk with God transcends marriage in intimacy.

- Marriage is more than sex.
  A happy marriage is much more than its bed.

- Sex is more than physiology.
  Sexual relations are much more than the sum of the anatomy involved.

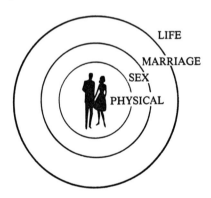

It is Related to Other Areas of Life

- Sex is the ultimate expression of the larger relationship of marriage. It affects and is shaped by all the circumstances and feelings involved in such a partnership.

- God intended that there be a background of sympathy, understanding, adoration, appreciation, and gentleness for the sexual relationship. The spiritual and soulish relationship is to be commensurate with the physical.

- This integration of sex into life distinguishes man from the sexual nature of animals, which is instinct without affection, biology without love.

- Marriage is a union of spirit, soul and body. In quantity of time, the physical aspect of marriage is far less important than the emotional, intellectual, and practical involvement of the couple. Thus, in preparation for marriage, the physical aspect of marriage needs no emphasis because it is the easiest and quickest area to learn, if the other areas of the relationship are in order.

- A good sexual relationship does not insure a good marriage but a good marriage insures a meaningful sexual relationship.

- Sex in marriage should never be an end in itself. If you treat your mate as an object of your sexual gratification, you are creating an intolerable climate for real love.

WHY DOES GOD CONFINE SEX TO MARRIAGE?

There are two kinds of answers to this question, one that focuses on the positive things that sex becomes in marriage, and the other on what negative things it becomes outside of marriage. Sexuality has the potential for good or evil, depending on motivation, expression, and timing.

The following are the positive reasons for confining sex to marriage:

- It is consistent with God's purpose and Word;

- It heightens its value;

- It represents the permanent, exclusive, unqualified commitment of marriage;

- It produces freedom between the sexes;

- It bases enjoyment on commitment;

- It makes intercourse the language of oneness;

- It permits sex to be the frosting rather than the foundation of relationship;

- It strengthens the relationship;

- It best prepares for real sharing with a real person.

The following are the negative results of sex outside of marriage:

- It hinders the development of the non-physical aspects of the relationship before and after the marriage;

- It makes a statement that is not true, implying a commitment that does not exist;

- It produces tension and guilt between the sexes;

- It has no guard against manipulation and self-centered motivation

- It can be idolatry and lead to deception and perversion

- It causes stagnation in the other areas of the relationship

- It hinders married sexual fulfillment

- It produces spiritual, mental, and emotional bondage

- It may lead to abortion, illegitimate births, and veneral disease.

Although some suggest sex outside of marriage to be beneficial even to marriage, we must accept God's ways as being best. We must avoid the fallacy of laying too much emphasis on the physical factors in marriage and recognize that pre-marital sex hinders dealing with the non-physical demands of marriage. The more sexually naive and inexperienced you are in coming to the marriage bed, the more eventual, reliable and mutual emotional and physical satisfaction there will be. Abstinence best prepares you for real sharing with a real person.

Sex is enjoyed in its fullest only under the auspices of a publicly acknowledged, permanent commitment. Public marriage is essential protection for the persons involved. It protects from the insecurity of a fickle partner. It protects society from relating to those persons as singles. It protects their offspring from the problems of illegitimacy and competition.

WHAT ARE SOME WRONG CONCEPTS OF SEX?

Sex is dirty and evil. This statement ignores the fact that sex was created by God before sin entered the human race *(Genesis 2,3)*. It is clean and holy in the sight of God when it is kept free from sin and lust.

Sex is shameful. This is contrary to the fact that God created sex to be beautiful and meaningful. Before sin entered, Adam and Eve were naked and not ashamed *(Genesis 2:24,25)*.

Sex is carnal. The members of our bodies can be instruments of righteousness or unrighteousness *(Romans 6:12-19)*. Our sexual life can be lived according to the flesh or according to the spirit. If it is lived according to the flesh, it will be compulsive, self-centered, and exploitative. If it is lived according to the spirit, it will be controlled, fulfilling, and mutually edifying.

Sex is for reproduction only. If design indicates purpose, then the Lord intended intercourse to be an experience of supreme pleasure. The Bible supports the view that sex is to be enjoyed whether conception takes place or not *(Proverbs 5:18,19; Ecclesiastes 9:9)*. The entire Song of Solomon also illustrates this delight *(Song 4:1-6; 7:1-9)*.

Sex is a drive equal to hunger and thirst. This is not true. Sex is more of an appetite. It is not automatic and irrepressible. The level of desire can and must be controlled. The sexual dimension is not a rampaging steam engine that must rely on safety valves. This is only true if the appetite is continually excited. Sex in marriage is meant to be an ongoing celebration, not a periodic safety valve.

Sex is a legal duty. This statement reflects not only a wrong concept but a wrong attitude. Sex is to be a joyful, loving privilege.

All physical affection is sexual. This is not true. The physical expression of affection shared by family members (e.g. father to daughter, mother to son, brothers and sisters) and close friends is not aimed at sexual union. We must not allow a worldly sex-consciousness to rob us of proper family affection *(I Kings 19:20; Romans 16:16; I Corinthians 16:20; II Corinthians 13:12; I Thessalonians 5:26; I Peter 5:14)*.

WHAT PRINCIPLES SHOULD GOVERN THE SEXUAL LIFE OF A CHRISTIAN COUPLE?

LOVE — Christian love is the greatest single factor contributing to a fulfilling sexual union. Love is having a greater desire to give than to receive. Both the husband and wife should desire to give and be willing to receive.

MEEKNESS — Meekness is yielding our personal rights and expectations to God. Much frustration in marriage is caused by expecting too much from our partner and reacting when they don't give us what we believe to be rightfully ours. Viewing God as the source of all fulfilment in life will free us to love each other unreservedly and to stand together through any difficulty.

COMMUNICATION — Based on love and meekness, any couple that is faithful to communicate will be able to find their way along the pathway of fulfilment. Failure to communicate clearly will only lead to frustration, hurt, resentment, and fear.

PURITY — The sexual life of a couple must be kept free from contaminating influences. Our hearts must be kept free from selfish desires, our minds from impure thoughts, and our lives from the world's sensual barrage.

CONTROL — Controlling our desires brings freedom and greater fulfilment. Control is not only essential during necessary times of abstinence in marriage, it is always a factor in releasing fulfilment.

SENSITIVITY — There is a constant need for both the husband and wife to be sensitive to each other's needs and desires. A servant's heart and plenty of personal consideration shown in all areas of marriage will contribute much to its success.

PREPARATION — Just as all important events in life receive special preparation, so should the sexual relationship of a couple. This should include thoughtfulness, cleanliness, a clear conscience, and positive attitudes. It may also require a change in wardrobe, improved personal habits, rest, and a lock on the bedroom door.

WHAT ARE SOME HELPFUL HINTS IN TEACHING CHILDREN ABOUT SEX?

• Concentrate on instilling proper values more than giving factual knowledge.

• Be approachable on the subject.

• Respond to their questions honestly without giving more in your answer than they really asked for.

• Don't project negative attitudes concerning the subject.

• Be careful not to arouse curiosity and promote undue interest.

• Build Biblical concepts, values, and attitudes throughout their lives, instead of waiting for one "big talk".

• Give yourself and your children the personal security that comes from the parents being the first ones to talk to their children about the subject. The street is not a good source for godly input.

FAMILY PROJECTS •

SECTION 2
LESSON 11
"Sex in Marriage"

"And these words which I command thee this day, shall be in thine heart: And thou shalt teach them diligently unto thy children and shalt talk of them when thou sittest in thine house, and when thou walkest by the way; and when thou liest down, and when thou risest up"
(Deuteronomy 6:6, 7).

Project One

☐ Set aside a special time alone for you and your spouse to discuss this lesson and its application to your life.

DATE ATTEMPTED: _____

RESULTS: _____

_____

_____

_____

Project Two

☐ If you have children, evaluate how you as parents are doing in instilling proper sexual concepts in them. Determine to make any adjustments that you feel are necessary.

DATE ATTEMPTED: _____

RESULTS: _____

_____

_____

_____

Finances in the Home

SCRIPTURE READING: I Timothy 6:6-11, 17-19;
Luke 12:16-31

The area of finances seems like such a "carnal" area and yet it certainly can be one of the major problems that can come between a married couple. Jesus placed a high priority on the right use of money in His teaching, considering the fact that two-thirds of all His parables deal with the subject of the right use of money.

WHAT ARE THE MAJOR FINANCIAL PROBLEMS THAT CAN DESTROY A MARRIAGE OR A FAMILY?

When we make the accumulation of wealth our ambition in life (Luke 12:16-31).

PROBLEM: This ambition can rob us of time and energy that we could be spending with our family.

• Fathers try to hold two jobs ("moonlight" in the evenings), or work extensive overtime depriving their families of quality time.

• Mothers are under pressure to go out of the home to get a job to supply additional income to fulfil desires.

SOLUTION: *I Timothy 6:6,* "Godliness with contentment is great gain". God does want us to accum-

ulate riches, but not material riches. Ask yourself, "Am I accumulating things because:"

• Others have influenced or pressured me to do it?

• I envy the lifestyle of those around me?

• I enjoy the sheer challenge of it?

• It makes me feel bigger in the eyes of others?

• I near the future?

All of these are wrong reasons. God wants us to place our confidence in Him and learn to be content with what we have *(Hebrews 13:5).*

When husband and wife have disagreements with regard to the use of excess funds.

PROBLEM: Since member of the family has a different perspective, set of priorities, and interests, they also have different ideas about where excess funds ought to be spent. Many times these viewpoints, interests, and priorities are based on a selfish desire to have the best for oneself.

SOLUTION: Make the determination for the use of excess funds a family project.

• Establish family goals for purchases over the year.

• Openly evaluate purchases with other members of the family on the basis of needs, wants, and desires *(I Timothy 6:8; Luke 3:10-14; I John 2:15-17).*

• Pray together about every major purchase, submitting to the will of God.

When there are large debts that must be paid.

PROBLEM: When there is a large accumulating debt, there is tremendous anxiety and pressure on the parents, and they cannot react properly to other family members.

Oftentimes excess debts are incurred because of:

• Over-indulgence — We spend a great deal on the luxuries of life that have no lasting value, such as eating out often, expensive entertainment, extravagant hobbies, sporting goods, etc. *(Proverbs 21:17).*

• Impulsive Buying — We buy things in a time of emotional stirring, with the money in our hand, not taking into account already committed funds.

• Shaky Investments — We lose money on "get rich quick" investments that rarely pay off *(Proverbs 28:20,22).*

• Slothfulness — We have difficulty working hard, therefore, we do not excel in our work and we are always seeking expensive luxuries that will eliminate work *(Proverbs 21:25-26).*

• Greediness — We are greedy in always desiring more than we have and always (almost boastfully) insisting on the best of everything *(Luke 12:15).*

• Covetousness — We are covetous of what we see others have, whether it be by watching our neighbors, our television, catalogues, or other advertising *(Psalm 73:2-3).*

• Materialistic Love — We feel that our love for our family must be proven by an extravagant bestowal of material things (i.e. Christmas, birthdays, etc.) not realizing that love is demonstrated in a life of loyalty and commitment.

• Unwise purchases — We buy because of sales pressure from low monthly payments without evaluating the total purchase (i.e. encyclopedias, pictures, cookware, etc.)

• Wrong use of credit — We use credit cards instead of money when they should be used primarily for convenience.

SOLUTION: Determine to live within your means *(Luke 3:14),* evaluate future purchases, and live a debt-free lifestyle.

WHAT ARE SOME POSITIVE STEPS TO FINANCIAL FREEDOM?

Realize that God is the Lord of your finances and possessions.

• He owns them *(Deuteronomy 10:14; Psalm 24:1).*

• He holds you accountable for them *(I Corinthians 4:1-2; Luke 16:11-12; Romans 14:12).*

• He is your provider *(Deuteronomy 8:17-18; Ecclesiastes 5:19).*

Adopt God's value system in your finances.

• Be sure you are putting God first through tithes and offerings *(Malachi 3:7-12; Proverbs 3:9-10).*

• Be sure your priority is on spiritual, permanent, and eternal things *(II Corinthians 4:18).*

Believe God to supply what you need.

• Through diligent labor *(Proverbs 10:4-6; 13:11; 12:14).*

• Through answered prayer *(Philippians 4:16; Hebrews 11:6; James 4:2).*

Develop sales resistance.

• Professional sales people are competing for your money. They will use every emotional and flesh-appealing technique possible. If you are not firm, ie, able to say 'no', then you are an easy prey.

• To avoid impulsive spending, ask these questions:

– Do we really need it? (Be honest now!)
– Is some other item more pressing than this one?
– Is the price reasonable?
– Is this the best time to buy?
– Have I checked and researched the item?
– Do I know the retailer's reputation?
– Are you sure no other item can be substituted?
– Does the retailer offer any "after the sale" services?

• To avoid impulsive grocery shopping:

– Stick to an itemized list from home;
– Use discount coupons;
– Shop alone, leaving dad and the kids at home;
– Remember that the last week of the month are the best buys;
– Don't shop when tired or hungry;
– Don't touch unless you want to buy;
– Don't wait to run out before you buy, use sale prices.

Carefully discern between needs and non-essentials (I Timothy 6:6-11).

• In the United States this is becoming harder to define all the time. If you are in a financial pinch, be hard on yourself.

• Pray about your wants. Maybe God wants someone to give you the desires of your heart instead of you paying cash for them.

• Remember that impulsive buying is the giant killer of the budget. Stay away from the stores and places that will tempt you. Know what you can afford and what you need. Everything else is out of bounds.

Make sure you take note of your failures in the past by asking yourself:

- Have I followed the Scriptural patterns?

- Do I have a way to control impulse buying?

- Is God trying to speak to me?

- Is God testing my faith?

- Am I setting my affections on the wrong things?

Make sure that you are willing to work toward the goal of financial freedom.

- Do not ignore outstanding debts *(Acts 24:16)*.

- Set a date in which to reach "Paid in Full".

- Be willing to make immediate sacrifice for long-term gain.

- Be willing to discipline and set guidelines for yourself.

SECTION 2
LESSON 12
"Finances in the Home"

"And these words which I command thee this day, shall be in thine heart: And thou shalt teach them diligently unto thy children and shalt talk of them when thou sittest in thine house, and when thou walkest by the way; and when thou liest down, and when thou risest up"
(Deuteronomy 6:6,7).

Project One ☐ Examine each of the areas listed on causes for over-indebtedness (Question C) and discuss how each family member can contribute to greater success in overcoming these areas.

DATE ATTEMPTED: _____

RESULTS: _____

_____

_____

Project Two ☐ Go to each member of the family and ask them the personal question: "What sacrifices are you willing to make to insure the success of the family in living within our means?"

DATE ATTEMPTED: _____

RESULTS: _____

_____

_____

Project Three ☐ Read *I Timothy 6:8; Luke 3:11* and *I John 2:15-16* and make your own definition of "needs" and "desires". Have each family member make up a list of his or her needs and desires, and a list of the needs and desires of each other family member.

DATE ATTEMPTED: _____

RESULTS: _____

_____

Handling Wealth and Abundance

SCRIPTURE READING: I Timothy 6

The dictionary defines "wealth" as "a large aggregate of real and personal property; an abundance of those material or worldly things that men desire to possess". It also states, "all material objects which have economic utility; all property possessing a monetary value" (Funk and Wagnalls).

HOW DOES GOD FEEL ABOUT WEALTH?

Wealth is a neutral term. It can be used in a positive way and a negative way. There is no particular virtue in God's eyes in a life of poverty nor is there any stigma attached to wealth. It is not our possession of money or lack of possession of money that determines our relationship to God, it is our attitude toward wealth that does. God is first of all concerned with our attitude toward money and possessions. With the rich fool, God did not object to his wealth, only to his use of it *(Luke 12:13-21).*

DOES GOD DESIRE HIS PEOPLE TO PROSPER?

Yes!

God not only desires that His people prosper, but He promises that they WILL prosper *(Psalm 1:3; 122:6, 7).*

True wisdom that comes to the people of God will produce riches and honor *(Proverbs 3:16-17; 8:18, 21).*

God has always desired blessing for His people *(Deuteronomy 28:1-14),* BUT, all of God's blessings are based on various conditions, which include:

- Obedience to God *(Deuteronomy 28:15-68; 19:9; Joshua 1:6-8; III John 2).*

- Placing God first *(Matthew 6:33; II Chronicles 31:21).*

- Diligence with what God has given you *(Proverbs 21:5; 24:30-34).*

WHY DOES GOD PROSPER HIS PEOPLE WITH ABUNDANCE?

To understand this, we must understand the principle of all ministry in the Body of Christ found in *II Corinthians 1:3-4.* The principle of all ministry in the Body of Christ is that God gives to us that we might become a channel of His blessing to others *(Ephesians 4:28).* This is exactly what God did with Abraham *(Genesis 12:1-3)*.

God blesses us with abundance that we might have to give to those who are in need *(I Timothy 6:8; 17-19; II Corinthians 8:1-15)*.

"And God is able to make all grace abound to you, that always having all sufficiency in everything you may have an abundance for every good deed, as it is written, 'He scattereth abroad, He gave to the poor, His righteousness abides forever'" *(II Corinthians 9:8-9 NAS)*.

"After all God can give you everything that you need, so thst you may always have sufficient both for yourselves and for giving away to other people" *(II Corinthians 9:8-9 Phillips)*.

WHAT ARE SOME WRONG ATTITUDES AND MOTIVATIONS FOR ACCUMULATING WEALTH?

God is more concerned about our attitudes and motives for accumulating wealth than He is about the wealth itself. Only God and the individual involved can know what his or her true motivation really is. Some of the wrong things that can motivate us are these:

- We are caught up in the spirit of the age *(I John 2:15-17)*.
- We are covetous *(Ps. 73:2-3; Luke 12:15)*.
- We enjoy the challenge *(Luke 12:18)*.
- It makes us feel important *(I Timothy 6:17)*.
- We feel more secure *(I Timothy 6:17-18; Proverbs 11:4,28)*.
- We love luxury *(I Timothy 6:8; Ecclesiastes 5:10)*.

WHAT ARE THE RIGHT MOTIVATIONS FOR ACCUMULATING WEALTH?

God has given us the pattern and example for every good and perfect thing that He expects us to do. When it comes to giving, God is the greatest and highest example. God, who is abundant in mercy, shows mercy *(Titus 3:4-7)*. God who is rich in grace, gives grace *(John 1:14-17)*. God who is full of love, extends His love *(John 3:16)*. God, who has everything at His disposal, has freely given to those who are in need *(II Corinthians 8:14-16; 9:6-15; James 1:5,17; John 3:16; Matthew 7:11)*.

The true motivation, then, for accumulating wealth, is so that we might have to give to those who are in need. This is clearly seen in the life of Joseph. Joseph was warned by God of a famine to come and was instructed by God to store up vast sums in big barns. He was given wisdom in the handling of the matter, BUT the purpose was so that in a time of need he would have to give to others *(Genesis 41:29-57)*.

HOW DOES GOD WANT US TO HANDLE FINANCIAL PROSPERITY?

God wants us to use every talent and possession that He has given to us for the glory of God and the exten-

sion of the Kingdom of God. Therefore the most valuable thing that we could do with the things He has given to us is to use them to make spiritual investments *(Matthew 25:14-30)*.

- We are to give to the poor *(Proverbs 22:9; Luke 12:33)*.
- We are to give to needy members of the Body of Christ *(II Corinthians 8:14; I John 3:17-18; James 2:15-17)*.
- We are to share with other family members *(I Timothy 5:8; Matthew 15:4-6)*.
- We are, at times, to open our hands to the unsaved *(Matthew 5:42; Luke 16:9-12)*.
- We are to give to the ministry *(I Timothy 5:17,18; I Corinthians 9:14)*.

This does not mean, however, that we are not to be discriminating in our giving *(II Thessalonians 3:10-15)*. There are many people that God may be correcting through the means of financial problems. For a well meaning Christian to interfere at this point may take the pressure off that God wants there to bring them to Him or to strengthen them. We must be careful in all of our giving to seek the mind of the Lord.

WHAT BIBLICAL UNDERSTANDING WILL HELP US KEEP A PROPER BALANCE IN THIS AREA OF WEALTH?

- Everything that we have comes from God and belongs to Him *(Genesis 39:3)*.

- True riches are not material but spiritual *(Proverbs 22:4; Luke 16:11; 12:21)*.

- The whole of the material world system is passing away *(II Peter 3:10-11)*.

- True satisfaction comes from being God-like *(Psalm 17:15)*.

- The greatest wealth is the Lord's blessing *(Proverbs 10:22; I Timothy 6:19)*.

- We are not to seek riches, but we are to seek God's kingdom *(Luke 12:31-34)*.

- When we give to the poor, we lend to the Lord and the Lord is a debtor to no man *(Proverbs 19:17; Luke 6:38)*.

Paul said: "I know both how to be abased, and I know how to abound: everywhere and in all things I am instructed both to be full and to be hungry, both to abound and to suffer need. I can do all things through Christ which strengtheneth me" *(Philippians 4:11-13)*.

God is wanting to teach His people how to abound so that when they do, it will not be to build their own barns bigger, but to extend the kingdom of God. Ask yourself, "CAN GOD TRUST ME WITH FINANCES?"

FAMILY   PROJECTS

SECTION 2
LESSON 13
"Handling Wealth and Abundance"

"And these words which I command thee this day, shall be in thine heart: And thou shalt teach them diligently unto thy children and shalt talk of them when thou sittest in thine house, and when thou walkest by the way; and when thou liest down, and when thou risest up"
(Deuteronomy 6:6,7).

Project One
☐ Discuss with your family each of the conditions for prosperity listed in the lesson under Question 2. Look up all of the scriptures and ask yourself the following questions in regard to each of these conditions. Do we measure up to this qualification? How could we better fulfill these qualifications?

DATE ATTEMPTED: _____

RESULTS: _____

_____

_____

Project Two
☐ For smaller children, read them the story in *Luke 13:16-21* and have them draw a picture about this story. After they are finished, have them explain their picture and tell what they have learned from the story.

DATE ATTEMPTED: _____

RESULTS: _____

_____

_____

Project Three
☐ Discuss with each family member ways in which they can individually set aside finances for reaching out to others. Make a specific decision in each case to take some decisive action in this regard.

DATE ATTEMPTED: _____

RESULTS: _____

_____

_____

14

Parental Responsibilities

SCRIPTURE READING: Deuteronomy 4

When God originally made man, there was something that was obviously incomplete about him. As man observed all the animals, each having male and female, he was made aware of his need for a help-meet in fulfilling God's charge to him *(Genesis 2:20)*. God did a miracle for this first man in building a woman to be with him and to help him fulfill God's charge. However, there was still a further dimension to be experienced by that first family. Eve was a wife and Adam was a husband, but they were soon to become the mother and father of us all. When they had children, they entered a whole new realm, the realm of parenthood *(Genesis 4:1-2)*.

WHAT IS THE IMPORTANCE OF PARENTS?

Parents are very important to God because:

Parents are the vessels through whom God desires to promote His eternal purpose in each family *(Genesis 1:26-28)*. Therefore:

- Parents are responsible to be fruitful and multiply.
- Parents are to aid in the production of godly character and maturity in the family members.
- Parents are to help bring forth God's deposit, potential, and ministry that He has placed in each child.
- Parents are to see that their children come to know and experience true fellowship with God.

Parents are the mediators of God's covenants to the family members and this means that the parents are to their children what the Lord is to them.

Ephesians 6:1 (Amplified Bible) says, "Children, obey your parents in the Lord (as His representatives), for this is just and right."

This teans that covenant benefits of the parents extend to the children *(Genesis 6:18; Exodus 20:5; Psalm 103:17,18; I Corinthians 7:14)*.

Because parents are so important to God as His instruments, God protects them even as He protects all leadership *(Exodus 21:17; Leviticus 19:3; 20:9; Ephesians 6:2)*.

WHAT ARE THE PRIVILEGES OF PARENTS?

Parents receive a special blessing from the Lord because they are able to see the fruit of their hands. Parents have the privilege of seeing that their children:

- Live a long life *(Deuteronomy 11:18-21)*

- Remember the Lord and walk in His ways *(Deuteronomy 4:9-10; 6:7-12; Exodus 12:24-27; Genesis 18:19).*

- Know God and are able to pass on the knowledge of God *(Psalm 78:5-6; Joel 1:3)*

WHAT ARE THE RESPONSIBILITIES OF PARENTS?

God has a great deal that He wants to accomplish through the ministry of the parents. However, these things will never be accomplished unless the parents take the responsibility that God has given to them. Parents are not free "to do their own thing", but they have been given specific responsibilities and charges by God. Parents are to give their children:

PROVISION (I Timothy 5:8; Matthew 18:6; II Corinthians 12:14)

- Provision for one's family includes more than just food, clothing, and housing. Parents are to provide in all areas of life including spiritual, emotional, social, intellectual, vocational, and moral areas.

PROTECTION (Ephesians 6:4)

- The parents are the ones who are responsible to guard the children and protect them from all the forces which would destroy the wholeness that God intended *(I Thessalonians 5:23).* They are to guard the children from sin, strife, idleness, worldliness, dishonesty, hate, moral impurity, and anything else that would cause them to become less than what God intended for them to be.

TRAINING (Proverbs 22:6)

- The parents are to spend their time training those God has placed under them. All parents train their children, but all do not train them in godliness. Parents train by their example *(Psalm 101:2-4),* by direct teaching *(Deuteronomy 4:9-10),* and by loving discipline *(Proverbs 13:24).* Children learn many things from their parents. They learn:
  - Attidues and values
  - How to respond to problems (theirs' and others')
  - How to respond to situations
  - How the parents respond to each other

GUIDANCE (Genesis 18:19)

- Parents are not just to sit back and let their children make their own way through life. They are to aid their children and equip their children in the decision-making

processes of life by contributing their wisdom and experience to them.

- When the parents take responsibility in all of these areas, they have truly provided a context and an environment that is conducive to godliness, change, and growth.

WHAT HAPPENS WHEN PARENTS FAIL TO TAKE THEIR RESPONSIBILITY?

Chaos and confusion prevail!
When parents fail to take their responsibility, they can expect their offspring to inherit curses instead of blessings *(Exodus 20:5; Leviticus 20:4-5; Isaiah 14:21-23; Jeremiah 9:14; Lamentations 5:7).* They can expect to raise a generation that will hate them and bring them to shame *(Proverbs 30:11-14; Proverbs 29:15).*

interesting

WHAT HAPPENS WHEN PARENTS FULFILL THE CHARGE THAT GOD HAS GIVEN TO THEM?

When parents have truly given themselves to the charge that God has given to them, they can epect God to reward them in special ways. God will turn the hearts of the children to the parents *(Malachi 4:6).* The children will rise up and call them blessed *(Proverbs 31:28).* Their children will truly be as olive plants about their table *(Psalm 128:3).*

"Blessed is every one that feareth the Lord; that walketh in His ways.

For thou shalt eat the labor of thine hands, happy shall thou be, and it shall be well with thee.

Thy wife shall be as a fruitful vine by the sides of thine house: thy children like olive plants round about the table. Behold, that thus shall the man be blessed that feareth the Lord.

The Lord shall bless thee out of Zion, and thou shalt see the good of Jerusalem all the days of thy life.

Yea, thou shalt see thy children's children, and peace upon Israel."

Ps. 128:1-6

FAMILY   PROJECTS

SECTION 3
LESSON 14
"Parental Responsibilities"

"And these words which I command thee this day, shall be in thine heart: And thou shalt teach them diligently unto thy children and shalt talk of them when thou sittest in thine house, and when thou walkest by the way; and when thou liest down, and when thou risest up"
(Deuteronomy 6:6,7).

Project One ☐ Have each member of the family write a paragraph answering the question, "Why are parents important?" After everyone has completed their paragraph, discuss the subject together. If you have small children, have them draw a picture.

DATE ATTEMPTED: _____

RESULTS: _____

_____

_____

_____

Project Two ☐ Have each family member tell what they appreciate most about their parents and have each of the children also indicate what they enjoy doing the most with their parents.

DATE ATTEMPTED: _____

RESULTS: _____

_____

_____

_____

15

Provision for the Family

SCRIPTURE READING: I Timothy 5:8; Matthew 18:6; II Corinthians 12:14

"If a man provide not for his household, he is worse than an infidel" *(I Timothy 5:8)*.

It is unmistakably clear that God expects parents to provide for their children. The most obvious question that comes to mind in assuming this responsibility is, "What are parents to provide?". Are parents only to provide food, clothing, and shelter? Is the child a self-developing person needing only the essential external supports to maintain life? If this were so, the State could supply these things and the parents could give themselves to 'more profitable' things, as they do in communist countries. Tragically enough though, in a country where parents say they believe their role is greater than just physical provisions, what they end up providing is far too often not much more than that.

WHAT RESPONSIBILITIES DO PARENTS HAVE TO THEIR CHILDREN IN THE AREAS OF PROVISION?

SPIRITUAL PROVISION

Spiritual provision comprises the ingredients necessary for a child to develop:

- Spiritual perspectives on life,
- God and others centered relationships,
- Christian (Biblical) behavior,
- Commitment to moral and ethical values.

EMOTIONAL PROVISION

Emotional provision is the sense of security that is given to the child by the appropriate balance of discipline, love, and encouragement *(Proverbs 22:6; Ephesians 6:4)*.

INTELLECTUAL PROVISION

Parents bear great responsibility in the education of their children *(Proverbs 22:6)*. A child's mind is like a blank piece of paper. The parents have the ultimate responsibility to oversee what is written on that paper. Almost 20% (one-fifth) of a child's life is spent in the first 12 years of school under the influence of others! Who is speaking into my child in the most formative years of his or her life? and What are they saying? are relevant questions for every parent to ponder. Am I aware of, and able to counteract any wrong influences in his/her life?

VOCATIONAL PROVISION

Parents are also responsible to see that their children receive the discipline and training that will equip them to take up a vocation, and do well at whatever they do *(Ecclesiastes 2:24; Proverbs 20:11; 6:6-11),* having specific career direction and good work habits.

SOCIAL PROVISION

Parents face a significant responsibility, too, in providing for the social development of the child both by example and training. This area includes:

- Principles of relationships: loving, serving, and forgiving *(Proverbs 19:26; 17:17)*
- Treatment of the opposite sex *(Proverbs 18:22; 21:9,19)*
- Hospitality
- Communication of thoughts and ideas *(Proverbs 18:19,20,21)*
- Good etiquette *(Proverbs 20:11)*

MORAL AND ETHICAL PROVISION

Parents must provide moral and ethical values for their children. By instruction and example, parents give to their children the morals and ethics that will promote and insure good relationships in society, the home, the Church, and the business world *(Matthew 6:25-34; Proverbs 3:1-4).*

Areas of moral and ethical provision:
- A strong sense of right and wrong *(Hebrews 1:9)*
- Proper business ethics *(Proverbs 11:1)*
- Social ethics *(I Corinthians 6)*
- Church ethics *(I Timothy 3:15)*

PHYSICAL PROVISION

Obviously, the most basic meaning of *I Timothy 5:8* is to provide for the physical or material needs of one's family.

Proverbs 31 tells us that the mother is also involved in this process. The physical/material supplies provide the basis for meeting all the other needs that have been mentioned.

How the parents go about this process (obtaining employment, spending the income, etc.) also speaks to the children as to how they will someday meet their own material and physical needs, as well as how they will do this for a family of their own.

HOW DO PARENTS GO ABOUT SUPPLYING THESE SPIRITUAL PROVISIONS?

Parents provide for their children the most influential life-model they will ever have. Through their good example, they set before their children the necessary spiritual provisions *(Proverbs 4:10,11)* in the areas of:

- Respect for authorities:
  - Parental
  - Civil
  - Ecclesiastical
- Value system
- Devotional patterns
- Love for God
- Ability to give to others
- Appreciation for the institution of marriage
- Concept of God
- Sense of responsibility for others
- Ability to solve problems
- Reality of Christianity: Does it work? If so, how?
- Opportunities for Christian service
- Environment conducive to spiritual growth.

Proverbs tells us that God expects parents to provide spiritual provisions by instruction *(Proverbs 1:8; II Timothy 3:15).*

Spiritual provisions are also supplied through relationship *(Proverbs 4:3,4).* It was the warm, responsive relationship that Solomon had with his father that enabled his father to give him great wisdom. This kind of relationship requires a great deal of time shared together.

FAMILY • PROJECTS •

SECTION 3
LESSON 15
"Provision for the Family"

"And these words which I command thee this day, shall be in thine heart: And thou shalt teach them diligently unto thy children and shalt talk of them when thou sittest in thine house, and when thou walkest by the way; and when thou liest down, and when thou risest up"
(Deuteronomy 6:6,7).

Project One ☐ Parents discuss between themselves how well they are doing in providing for the spiritual, social, intellectual, emotional, moral, vocational, and physical needs of the children.

DATE ATTEMPTED: _____

RESULTS: _____

_____

_____

_____

Project Two ☐ Discuss with the children what they believe their greatest needs are. Have small children draw a picture of some of the things Mom and Dad have provided.

DATE ATTEMPTED: _____

RESULTS: _____

_____

_____

_____

16

Protection for the Family

SCRIPTURE READING: Genesis 6-8; Hebrews 11:7

WHY IS IT NECESSARY FOR PARENTS TO PROTECT THEIR CHILDREN?

BECAUSE THEIR CHILDREN ARE VALUABLE:

We protect most what we value most. Anything that is valuable needs protection. The possessions that we value most, we safeguard to insure our continued possession of them. The most valuable possessions that parents have are their children, therefore, we should give them the greatest protection possible. Our protection of them is the proof of our love for them *(Psalm 128:3)*.

BECAUSE THEIR CHILDREN ARE DAMAGEABLE:

Just as the tender young plant needs special protection from the destructive forces in the open field, so a child must be sheltered from receiving the full-force of the storms of life. A child is more vulnerable to damaging influences than an adult, therefore must be guarded from them *(Psalm 144:12)*.

BECAUSE THEIR CHILDREN ARE CORRUPTIBLE:

Just as foods must be preserved from spoiling, so a child must be protected from the corruptive elements within and around him. Sinful attitudes within a child must be dealt with, or they will eventually destroy him *(Proverbs 22:15)*.

FROM WHAT ARE PARENTS TO PROTECT THEIR CHILDREN?

PHYSICAL HARM:

Parents are to oversee the growth of their children's bodies by not only providing nourishment, but by also doing their best to keep them from sickness and danger. This can be done by giving them a balanced diet, by promoting good sleep and exercise habits, by training them in personal hygiene, by teaching safety precautions, and by instilling in them obedience to authority. In *Genesis 45:7* God showed His concern for the physical well-being of the family. It is only natural that parents guard their children from dangers *(Luke 11:11-13)*.

SOCIAL ABUSE:

A child's mind and emotions can be greatly damaged by the abusive treatment of other people. Parents should do their best to protect their children from any extreme abuses of this kind. To do this the parent should monitor the kind of people their children are around, as well as realize the influence they have on them *(Psalm 140:1,4,; 31:20; Matthew 18:6).*

EVIL ASSOCIATIONS:

A child should not be allowed to associate with any person bent on leading them into sinful activities *(Psalm 12:7; Proverbs 2:11-16; 1:10-19; I Corinthians 15:33).*

CORRUPTING INFLUENCES:

A child should not be exposed to things that will corrupt his values, attitudes, or behavior, for instance, non-Christian teachers, television, movies, music, and certain reading material. *(John 17:11-15; II Thessalonians 3:3; Romans 16:19; Proverbs 19:27).*

SPIRITUAL FORCES:

A child should be consistently covered by his parents' prayers. Powerful spiritual forces are out to ensnare children as well as adults *(Job 1:5).*

SINFUL ATTITUDES:

As a child grows, sinful attitudes will be expressed from his heart. He should be protected from them by having them dealt with through instruction and discipline *(Proverbs 22:15).*

HOW CAN PARENTS PROTECT THEIR CHILDREN?

BY INVOLVEMENT:

Parents need to be involved in their children's lives to know what affect different influences are having upon them. They need to be able to sense when their child is in danger. Children will tend to be more responsive to the covering of a parent who is involved in their lives *(Proverbs 29:15).*

BY DISCERNMENT:

Parents need to be able to determine what influence a potential involvement will have on their children. They need to be able to discern problems before they develop *(Proverbs 2:11)* by asking God for special wisdom *(James 1:5-7).*

BY COMMUNICATION:

In that covering is primarily relational, communication is a key factor in its effectiveness. Continual communication will make times of stress and danger easier to handle *(Proverbs 1:8; 2:1; 3:1; 4:1,10,20; 5:1; 6:1; 7:1).*

BY EXAMPLE:

The parents' own avoidance of harmful influences will teach the child safe ways to live. Even though not wanting to, children will often fall into the same snares as their parents *(Exodus 20:5,6; Lamentations 5:7).*

BY INSTRUCTION:

The Book of Proverbs reveals that parents should not only teach their children right ways to live, but should also warn them of the wrong ways, exposing error *(Proverbs 6:32,33; 7:22,23,27).*

BY RESTRICTION:

Parents have and must exercise the authority to restrict their children from dangerous involvements. This gives the child the advantage of the parent's wisdom and experience *(Proverbs 6:20-26; Deuteronomy 6:24).*

BY DISCIPLINE:

The protection of children is so important that God has ordained that parents even utilize discipline and force to persuade their children to submit to their restrictions. The lesser pain of discipline is to prevent the greater pain of destruction *(Proverbs 23:13,14).*

BY REPLACEMENT:

Parents should not only restrict their children from harmful involvements, they should replace them with positive alternatives. Making that which is helpful available, will deter the choice of that which is harmful *(Romans 12:21).*

FAMILY PROJECTS

SECTION 3
LESSON 16
"Provision for the Family"

"And these words which I command thee this day, shall be in thine heart: And thou shalt teach them diligently unto thy children and shalt talk of them when thou sittest in thine house, and when thou walkest by the way; and when thou liest down, and when thou risest up"
(Deuteronomy 6:6,7).

Project One

☐ After discussing the content of this lesson as a family, ask your children to give you ways in which they want to be protected by you.

DATE ATTEMPTED: _____

RESULTS: _____

_____

_____

_____

Project Two

☐ Take a special time as parents to evaluate how well you are doing in protecting your family in the areas listed under Question 2. Ask yourselves questions like: Who is influencing my children? What are they learning? What is affecting their attitudes, words, and actions? Do we need to make any adjustments?

DATE ATTEMPTED: _____

RESULTS: _____

_____

_____

_____

17

Training Children by Example

SCRIPTURE READING: Deuteronomy 6

The goal of training children is to bring them to a level of maturity whereby they might be able to make responsible decisions on their own, resulting in responsible actions that reflect the right values and attitudes of the parents.

WHAT DOES IT MEAN TO "TRAIN"?

Websters defines training as "guiding the growth of; guiding the mental, moral, etc., development of; to bring up; to rear; to discipline or condition; to prepare to make fit."

Ephesians 6:4 says parents are to "bring (children) up in the nurture and admonition of the Lord."

The phase "bring . . . up . . . " means to "rear up to maturity; to cherish or train". God wants us to bring our children to the place of maturity through daily training *(Deuteronomy 6:7)*.

WHY IS IT NECESSARY FOR PARENTS TO TRAIN THEIR CHILDREN?

• Children are sinners. It is very important for parents to "train" them to discern between right and wrong and to prepare them for the new birth experience *(Psalm 51:5)*.

• Children are ignorant. The principles and concepts imparted to them from the youngest age will make up their understanding and frame of reference *(Proverbs 19:2)*.

• Children are imitators. The lifestyle and habits of parents will be transmitted to their children *(Ezekiel 16:44)*.

• Children are vulnerable. They need to be trained to beware of the dangers of life *(Matthew 10:16; 18:6)*.

• Children are potentiality. A well-trained, disciplined person can achieve great success in life. God has a purpose and a plan for your children that can only be fully realized as you cooperate in training them.

• Children are transmitters. The Christian faith and lifestyle is passed down through the generators as parents train their children in the ways of the Lord *(Psalm 78:4-8; Psalm 145:4)*.

HOW DO PARENTS TRAIN THEIR CHILDREN IN THE WAYS OF THE LORD?

The passage from Deuteronomy, chapter 6 (verses 5-7) gives us clear insight into the methods of training our children.

- "Thou shalt love the Lord thy God". Parents themselves must have a demonstrated love for God in every area of their personal life.

  - "heart"
  - "soul"
  - "might"

- "These words shall be in thine heart". God's principles must be a part of every parent's life. A father and a mother must know God's Word personally and be able to share it. This necessitates attending church, receiving teaching, reading, and studying the scriptures and applying God's principles daily.

- "Thou shalt teach (these words) diligently unto thy children". It is a divinely established responsibility of parents to constantly give positive scriptural input into the hearts and minds of their children. Parents are to verbalize God's words continually:

  - "When thou sittest in thine house" includes family time and times of relaxation.
  - "When thou walkest by the way" includes times of transportation or walking.
  - "When thou liest down" means at bed time.
  - "When thou risest up", means in the morning.

It is obvious in this passage that the predominant means for training up children in the ways of the Lord is the lifestyle of the parents.

We can only train our children to be waht we ourselves already are. "Like begets like". We are compelled to examine closely our lifestyle and consider whether or not we are properly serving our children as adult models of the Christian way of life *(I Corinthians 4:16; 11:1; I Timothy 4:16; II Timothy 3:10,11,14)*.

IN WHAT ARE PARENTS TO TRAIN THEIR CHILDREN?

The training of children relates to every part of life. Listed below are some primary areas in which proper training is essential for success in life.

VALUES:

☐ Is the way I'm handling my money teaching my children Biblical values?

☐ Is the way I'm using my time training my children to put God first?

ATTITUDES:

☐ Is my attitude towards authority teaching my children to respond whole-heartedly to God's delegated authority?

☐ Does my outlook on life inspire positive attitudes in my children?

☐ Do I demonstrate the kind of love that teaches my children to love as God does?

☐ Does my attitude of meekness teach my children to yield their rights to God?

RIGHT WORDS:

☐ Does my daily language consistently teach my children to communicate in an edifying manner?

☐ Do my words of commendation encourage and motivate my children to more good works?

BEHAVIOR AND GODLY HABITS:

☐ Does my behavior teach my children something different than my words?

☐ Are my children learning self-control by my balanced lifestyle?

FRIENDS:

☐ Does my circle of friends teach my children how to choose and develop proper friendships?

☐ Am I reaching out to others and thereby teaching my children to enlarge their circle of friends?

WISDOM:

☐ Am I teaching my children wisdom and good judgment by making daily decisions based on the principles of God?

☐ Does my response to my failures teach my children how to learn from their own?

☐ Do I relate God's Word to experiences and circumstances in daily situations in my home?

PHYSICAL HEALTH:

☐ Does my general physical condition motivate my children to keep themselves in good health?

It is vital that parents examine each of these areas in their own personal lives and evaluate whether or not their lifestyle would be desirable to be passed on to their children.

Evaluate the above areas and check the ones in which you as a parent feel that you are being a consistent godly example.

• FAMILY PROJECTS •

SECTION 3
LESSON 17
"Training Children by Example"

"And these words which I command thee this day, shall be in thine heart: And thou shalt teach them diligently unto thy children and shalt talk of them when thou sittest in thine house, and when thou walkest by the way; and when thou liest down, and when thou risest up"
(Deuteronomy 6:6,7).

Project One

☐ Discuss with your family what it means to love God with *all* your "heart, soul, and might". What are some practical ways in which this is done?

DATE ATTEMPTED: _____

RESULTS: _____

_____

_____

Project Two

☐ As a father and mother, practise verbalizing God's principles during the four times of the day (see Question #3). *Record the response of these attempts.*

DATE ATTEMPTED: _____

RESULTS: _____

_____

_____

Project Three

☐ As parents, analyze some of the traits your children have picked up from you, and begin working on the negative ones and reinforcing the positive ones with praise.

DATE ATTEMPTED: _____

RESULTS: _____

_____

_____

18

Training Children by Instruction

SCRIPTURE READING: Proverbs 1:1-19

Perhaps the most difficult area for parents to assume their responsibility in raising their children is the area of instruction. Feelings of inadequacy, misunderstanding of parental teaching responsibility, over-dependency on educational institutions, and improper values may all undermine a parent's sense of responsibility for the life education of their children. Many parents feel that living an exemplary life coupled with sending their children to the right schools will ensure a good upbringing for their children. However, though these are very important, nothing can replace in a child's life the value of the personal instruction of their parents.

WHAT DOES IT MEAN TO INSTRUCT OUR CHILDREN?

• A dictionary definition of the word 'instruct' is "to teach, train or educate; to give directions, or to inform". The word teach means: "to show or help to learn how to do something, to cause to know or understand."

• The words used in Scripture for teaching or instruction mean "to cause to understand; to admonish; to chasten; to reprove, to warn; to restrain; to point out; to enlighten; to cause to ascertain by seeing; to educate; to disciple; and to indoctrinate."

• As parents we are to give our children a basic life education to prepare them for the responsibilities of adult life. We are to impart to them what we have personally learned in life as well as oversee their educational experiences.

WHAT DOES THE BIBLE SAY ABOUT PARENTAL INSTRUCTION?

Deuteronomy 4:1-40

Prental instruction is the key to the success of the next generation. Parents are to teach their children and grandchildren.

Deuteronomy 6:7

Parents are to be diligent in teaching their children the commandments of God.

Deuteronomy 11:18-21

Parents are to be continually teaching their children the Word of God.

Proverbs 1:8

"My son, hear the instruction of thy father, and forsake not the law of thy mother."

Proverbs 4:1

"Hear, ye children, the instruction of a father."

Proverbs 13:1

"A wise son heareth his father's instruction."

Proverbs 15:5

"A fool despiseth his father's instruction."

Proverbs 19:27

"Cease, my son, to hear the instruction that causeth to err from the words of knowledge."

Proverbs 23:22

"Hearken unto thy father that begat thee, and despise not thy mother when she is old."

I Corinthians 4:14-21

Paul's role as a spiritual father included instruction.

Ephesians 6:4

Fathers are to raise their children in the nurture (education) and admonition (confrontation) of the Lord.

IN WHAT ARE PARENTS TO INSTRUCT THEIR CHILDREN?

IN THE REALM OF KNOWLEDGE

Parents are responsible to pass on to their children facts and information in all the basic areas of life. This should include areas such as natural life, spiritual life, people, nature, communication, finances, and social customs.

IN THE REALM OF UNDERSTANDING

Parents are responsible to impart insight into life to their children. This would include explaining the reasons why things happen and how things work.

IN THE REAL OF WISDOM

Parents are responsible to develop in their children the ability to make right decisions. This includes developing skill in various areas of life as well as learning how to use knowledge rightly.

HOW CAN PARENTS INSTRUCT THEIR CHILDREN?

BY DEVELOPING A MEANINGFUL DEVOTIONAL TIME

Different ways of Bible reading, Bible memorization, sharing, singing, discussion, and prayer can be used to teach children eternal truth.

BY LEARNING FROM THE LIVES OF OTHERS

Storytelling, dramatization, books, and even homemade tapes can be effective ways of gleaning wisdom from the experiences of others.

BY TURNING THE CIRCUMSTANCES OF LIFE INTO LEARNING EXPERIENCES

Perplexing situations, failures, successes, joys, and sorrows are all golden opportunities to impart wisdom and understanding. This is true for situations being faced by the children, the parents or both.

BY USING QUESTIONS

The many questions that children ask are openings for learning. These should be handled sincerely so as to create a greater openness. Parents can also ask questions to create curiosity.

BY SHARING YOUR LEARNING EXPERIENCES

The lessons learned by you and your family should become like family treasures handed down from generation to generation.

BY INVOLVING THEM IN THINGS YOU DO

Whether it is work, hobbies, household chores, or recreation, your children will enjoy doing it with you and will be open to learning through it.

BY WORKING ON PROJECTS TOGETHER

Study projects, experiments, making or putting things together, or even including educational experiences on vacations are ways of gaining knowledge together.

BY CREATING A HOME ATMOSPHERE CONDUCIVE TO LEARNING

Music, games, reading material, pictures, plaques, T.V., and radio can all be used to produce an environment to stimulate learning.

FAMILY • PROJECTS •

SECTION 3
LESSON 18
"Training Children by Instruction"

"And these words which I command thee this day, shall be in thine heart: And thou shalt teach them diligently unto thy children and shalt talk of them when thou sittest in thine house, and when thou walkest by the way; and when thou liest down, and when thou risest up"
(Deuteronomy 6:6,7).

Project One ☐ Evaluate together (either with or without your children) how you are doing in teaching your children. List areas in which you need to be instructing them. Use the points listed under Question #4 in the lesson to determine ways you can do better.

DATE ATTEMPTED: _____

RESULTS: _____

_____

_____

_____

Project Two ☐ Have a family learning night. Let the children decide (within your limitations) something they would like to learn about and then plan a creative evening of learning together.

DATE ATTEMPTED: _____

RESULTS: _____

_____

_____

19

Training Children By Discipline (Part I)

SCRIPTURE READING: Hebrews 12:1-29

Parents are given a charge by God to train their children. Part of that training involves the exercise of discipline. In order to receive the desired results, however, we must be sure that we are following the godly pattern.

WHERE DO WE HAVE THE PATTERN FOR ALL DISCIPLINE?

God Himself as our Heavenly Father furnishes the best and primary example of all discipline *(Deuteronomy 8:5)*.

- God chastens His children out of love *(Jeremiah 10:24; Proverbs 3:11-12; 13:24; Revelation 3:19)*.

- God chastens because He is faithful to us *(Psalm 119:75)*.

- God chastens as a form of instruction in His law *(Psalm 94:12)*.

- God chastens but afterward re-establishes His love to us *(Job 5:18; Jeremiah 31:18-20; Psalm 89:32-33)*.

WHAT ARE THE PURPOSES OF GOD THE FATHER'S DISCIPLINE?

God never disciplines His children to avenge or vindicate Himself. He only disciplines for the good of His children.

- To keep them from going astray *(Psalm 119:67; Hosea 7:11-12; Jeremiah 10:23-24)*.

- To keep them from the calamity of the wicked *(Psalm 94:12,13; I Corinthians 11:32)*.

- To draw them closer to Himself *(Isaiah 26:16)*.

- To make them wise *(Proverbs 22:15)*.

- To bring them into the experience of life *(Hebrews 12:9)*.

- To produce righteousness and holiness in them *(Hebrews 12:10-12; Malachi 3:3)*.

- To teach them the right ways of God *(Psalm 119:71)*

- To produce greater fruitfulness in their lives *(John 15:2)*.

WHY IS THE DISCIPLINING OF CHILDREN NECESSARY?

• Children are born in sin and naturally gravitate toward the exercise of self-will *(Psalm 51:5; Ephesians 2:3; Prov. 22:15)*.

• Children do not know that which is right *(Jeremiah 10:23)*.

• Children left to themselves will not fulfill God's purpose in their lives, but they will bring shame to their parents *(Proverbs 29:15)*.

• Children who have learned through discipline to respond to the authorities in their lives will also respond to the voice of the Lord *(Proverbs 23:13,14)*.

WHAT IS THE PRIMARY CAUSE FOR THE EXERCISE OF DISCIPLINE?

Disobedience.

• God brought discipline to His children when they failed to obey His commands, statutes, precepts, and ordinances *(Isaiah 42:24-25; Leviticus 26:27-28)*. When we walk in a way contrary to God's commands, we can expect to be chastened by Him.

• Parents of children are also to discipline for the primary cause of disobedience *(Ephesians 6:1-3; Deuteronomy 30:2; Colossians 3:20)*.

• They are not to discipline out of personal frustration.

• They are not to discipline out of wrath or anger *(Jeremiah 10:24; Ephesians 6:4; Colossians 3:21)*.

• They are not to discipline out of a personal discomfort caused.

WHAT IS TO BE THE RESPONSE TO GODLY DISCIPLINE?

It is possible to respond improperly to discipline. Parents can respond improperly to the discipline of the Lord and children can respond improperly to the discipline of their parents *(Jeremiah 2:30; 5:3; Haggai 2:17; Proverbs 15:10)*.

If children, however, have a proper understanding of godly discipline, they will:

• Be happy *(Job 5:17)*
• Not despise it *(Hebrews 12:5-6; Job 5:17-18*
• Embrace it *(Proverbs 15:10)*
• Endure it and learn what they are to learn from it *(Hebrews 12:7)*
• Repent and turn with zeal to the ways of God *(Revelation 3:19)*

SECTION 3
LESSON 19

*"Training
Children by Discipline"
(Part I)*

*"And these words which I command thee this day, shall be
in thine heart: And thou shalt teach them diligently unto
thy children and shalt talk of them when thou sittest in
thine house, and when thou walkest by the way; and when
thou liest down, and when thou risest up"*

(Deuteronomy 6:6,7).

Project One

☐ Parents, share with your children an example of how God disciplined you in
your life and what was the result.

DATE ATTEMPTED: _____

RESULTS: _____

_____

_____

Project Two

☐ Have different members of the family answer "how" questions based on the
answers to Question #2 in the lesson. For example:
• How has the discipline kept me from going astray?
• How has discipline kept me from the calamity of the wicked?
• How has discipline drawn me closer to the Lord?

DATE ATTEMPTED: _____

RESULTS: _____

_____

_____

Project Three

☐ Have each family member (including parents) discuss how they generally
respond to discipline and ways inwhich they could improve.

DATE ATTEMPTED: _____

RESULTS: _____

_____

_____

Training Through Discipline (Part II)

WHAT IS THE GODLY PRESCRIPTION FOR DISCIPLINING IN THE HOME?

• Make sure that your discipline is motivated by love and concern for the child, not anger.

• Make sure that your discipline is administered with a view to instruction and training your child in the right ways of God, not just stopping the wrong.

• Make sure that you have laid the proper groundwork for discipline. Before correcting a child, ask yourself the following questions:

–Have I ever given them specific guidelines in this area?

Before we can discipline our children for wrong behavior, we must be sure that we have taught them what we expect. They must have truth to draw upon. They must know what is expected of them. God always gave instruction to His people before He held them accountable.

–Have I made my instructions clear and understandable to their level?

When we give instructions to our children, we cannot take for granted that they know all the things that we know. We must make sure that we show them exactly what we expect. We must be careful to communicate it on their level, otherwise their error may be a sin of ignorance. Have them repeat your instructions to you to make sure they understand.

–Am I being reasonable in my request of them?

When parents ask their children to do things, many times they expect things from their children that they are not mature enough handle. The child may respond by acting silly or childish. Parents must be sure that their children are able to handle their requests.

–Have I been consistent in the treatment of this area?

If parents are inconsistent in their discipline in an area, the child will be insecure, never knowing when the parent is ready to back his word up with discipline. In such a case, the child's disobedience may be the fault of the parent.

• Make sure that you follow certain basic guidelines.

Many of these guidelines apply specifically to small children, but the principles behind them apply to all ages.

–Do not wait until a child's behavior is wrong to teach correct behavior.

• If the parent has not taught truth, all he can do is wait until wrong behavior arises and react to it.

• A child learns security when he has basic truths to guide him.

–Be in agreement with your spouse before you discipline.

–Never use humiliation as a means of correction.
• Never embarrass a child by disciplining in public.
• Never call them names (stupid, nit-wit, brat, etc.)
• Never talk down to them.
• Never attack the child, attack the problem!

–Teach them that "no" means "no".
• Don't continually warn them. At the most you should only give one warning and that is in cases where they may not have understood the command.
• Don't threaten your children, especially in regard to things you have no intention of fulfilling (i.e. ringing neck, slap silly, etc.)

–Never raise your voice in instruction or command.

–Establish your child's personal responsibility. Have them tell you what they did wrong.
• Don't ask, "Did you do that?" You will give them opportunity to lie.
• Don't ask, "Why did you do that?" You will encourage them to compose an excuse.
• Ask, "What did you do that was wrong?"

–Explain again to the child the reason for discipline.

–Sit in silence a few moments before you correct for their personal reflection.

–Correct with a rod, a neutral object *(Proverbs 23:13,14)*.
• Never correct with your hand. Use your hands to show love.
• Never use the "eye for eye" method (i.e., bitting them, pulling their hair, or scratching them.)

–Apply the board of education to the seat of knowledge.
• God has provided the perfect place for discipline to avoid injury.
• Never slap in face, or on hands, or anywhere else on the body.

–Correct firmly and do not let their crying stop you *(Proverbs 20:30; 19:18)*
• The child must associate wrong doing with pain.

–Do not over-correct. Use no more discipline than is necessary.
• Hard spanking and consistency of spanking break the will, not the length of the spanking.

–Show love without nullifying discipline.

–Do not degrade the child but encourage them in right behavior patterns.

–Pray with your child and help them to pray for forgiveness.

–If there is a need for restitution, have the child follow through.

–Be consistent!

WHAT ARE SOME ADDITIONAL GUIDELINES THAT WOULD APPLY TO OLDER CHILDREN?

There is a time when older children are too big to spank. Some of the following guidelines may be helpful:

• Discipline by the removal of certain privileges.

–Send them to bed early.
–Limit their privileges.
–**Never** take them out of church activities as a means of discipline.

• Provide additional motivation by rewarding correct behavior.

–Allow them special privileges (activities at school, sports, group activities).
–Give them more areas of responsibility.
–Put them in situations where they can begin proving themselves.

• Take time for heart-to-heart communication.

–Spend time in developing a good relationship.
–Be sure to express displeasure toward wrong doing.
–Be sure to give praise for right behavior.

When parents have entered into a good relationship with their children, by the time their children grow up, the most effective tool is the approval or disapproval of the parent. If the relationship does not exist between the parents and the children, time must be given to the children so that this relationship can develop, otherwise the children will be affected more by their immature peers, neighbors, or friends instead of their parents.

FAMILY PROJECTS

SECTION 3
LESSON 20
"Training Children by Discipline" (Part II)

"And these words which I command thee this day, shall be in thine heart: And thou shalt teach them diligently unto thy children and shalt talk of them when thou sittest in thine house, and when thou walkest by the way; and when thou liest down, and when thou risest up"
(Deuteronomy 6:6,7).

Project One ☐ As parents, sit down and discuss the material in this lesson and evaluate their own procedures. Concentrate on areas of weakness in your present means of discipline. Make some fresh determinations in regard to the future.

DATE ATTEMPTED: _____

RESULTS: _____

_____

_____

_____

Project Two ☐ As parents, read this lesson to your children and ask them if they think that there are any ways in which they think they could improve in areas of discipline.

DATE ATTEMPTED: _____

RESULTS: _____

_____

_____

_____

21

Providing Guidance for your Children

SCRIPTURE READING: Proverbs 4

From the day that a child first arrives in the home, parents are preparing them to leave. This will either be done by intelligent design or the lack of it. God has given every parent approximately eighteen years in which to plant in their children the wisdom, intelligence, and know-how to face life in such a way that honors God, contributes to society, blesses the church, and, as a by-product, meets the deep needs of that individual.

Guidance is an extremely important part of that preparation process. Parents institute by their actions the whole idea of guidance. The child in later life will often fail to seek guidance if his role models stated that it was unnecessary by their example.

WHAT IS GUIDANCE?

A guide is someone who leads or directs another in his way. It can be something that provides a person with directional information or signposts. A guide directs a person in his conduct or course of life.

Guidance is the act or process of leading or directing. It can include the process of controlling the course of a projectile by a built-in mechanism. Parents must build God's law into the inner-most being of their children *(Psalm 51:6).*

WHY IS GUIDANCE NECESSARY FOR CHILDREN?

• To keep them from destruction *(Proverbs 2:16-22; Matthew 6:13)* and wandering *(Ephesians 4:14).*

• To insure them the promise of spiritual blessing *(Isaiah 58:11; John 16:13; Psalm 139:24)*

HOW DOES GOD GIVE DIRECTION AND GUIDANCE TO HIS CHILDREN?

The pattern for man in relation to his children is given by God in his relationship to us. There are four basic ways God has designed for His children to receive the wisdom that is necessary in order to make right choices in life.

BY INSTRUCTION:

God instructed Adam and Eve as to the path of life *(Genesis 3:1-3; 2:16-17; Proverbs 1:8,9; 4:11-13).*

BY EXPERIENCE:

God gave opportunity for Adam and Eve to learn by experience *(Genesis 3:1-6,22; cf. 30:27).*

BY FAILURE:

God showed Adam and Eve the cause and effect relationship between sin and the curse *(Genesis 3:14,17).*
- Regarding personal failure *(cf. Proverbs 15:31,32)*
- *Regarding failure of others (cf. Proverbs 24:30-34)*

BY EXAMPLE:

God provided, Adam and Eve the example that they were to follow by virtue of who He was *(Genesis 3:5,22; II Corinthians 6:14-18).*

IN WHAT WAYS DO PARENTS PROVIDE THEIR CHILDREN WITH COUNSEL AND GUIDANCE?

BY INSTRUCTION: (Proverbs 5:1-2,7; 4:1-6)

Parents instruct their children on what choices are right and what choices are wrong. They also provide for them *how* to make right choices by judging and analyzing a situation according to God's Word.

BY EXPERIENCE:

Parents provide opportunities for their children to gain from life experiences by giving them the responsibility of making some of their own choices in areas of personal freedom. Discussing the results of their choices in areas such as use of finances, use of time, selection of friends, etc. provides extremely relevant guidance that they can use for the rest of their lives.

BY FAILURE:

One of the most valuable forms of guidance that a parent can share with his/her child is the account of some of his/her own personal failures, the results of those failures, and what he/she has learned through them. Parents can also provide guidance by discussion of the failures of others. This kind of discussion has a Biblical base. Many Biblical accounts are of failures, not in a gossiping manner, but as signposts of the wrong route to go in a specific area of life.

BY EXAMPLE:

Parents also provide guidance through their own example. Parental right choices automatically lead the child to do the same. The process of seeking counsel in various areas on the part of parents leads the child to believe that one does not always lean on his own narrow viewpoint, that in the multitude of counselors there is wisdom. Parents should ask family members, from time to time, what their opinion is on certain matters. This creates an openness to receive from others.

IN WHAT AREAS DO CHILDREN NEED GUIDANCE?

IN SOCIAL AREAS:

- The selection of friends
- The principles of relating to people
- The process of mending relationships
- The ability to conduct oneself publicly
- The ability to solve problems
- The choice of a marriage partner

IN SPIRITUAL AREAS:

- The blessing of right choices
- How to make the Bible relate to life
- The folly of wrong choices
- Direction in ministry involvement
- How to receive direction from God
- How to lead others to Christ and into righteous living
- How to build a good relationship with God through prayer

IN PERSONAL AREAS:

- The use of time
- How to maintain good health
- How to view oneself
- How to handle fear of the future

IN VOCATIONAL AREAS:

- How to enjoy your work
- How to choose a career
- How to find a job
- How to decide the if's and where's of attending college
- How to discipline oneself in school and work
- How to avoid becoming a workaholic

IN MORAL AREAS:

- How to handle one's thought life
- What sex is all about (appropriate to age-level)
- How to recognize and avoid moral pitfalls

IN FINANCIAL AREAS:

- What place money has in life
- How to spend money wisely
- How to save money
- How much to tithe and give in offerings
- How to avoid or get out of debt
- What to think and do about credit
- What charitable contributions should and should not be made

IN PHYSICAL AREAS:

- The value of recreation
- How to maintain self-discipline in eating habits
- The obvious follies of drug and alcohol use

The focus of guidance in the home is on values and methods. From birth to marriage, the parents provide guidance as to the right value system and the specific practical steps on how to reach any valuable objective. Parents are the chief source of counsel for their children. Parents cannot afford to leave that responsibility to others. Neither should they always wait for their child to come to them to ask for it.

• FAMILY PROJECTS •

SECTION 3
LESSON 21
"Providing Guidance for your Children"

"And these words which I command thee this day, shall be in thine heart: And thou shalt teach them diligently unto thy children and shalt talk of them when thou sittest in thine house, and when thou walkest by the way; and when thou liest down, and when thou risest up"
(Deuteronomy 6:6,7).

Project One ☐ Have father share some personal experience of guidance from his own life with all the thoughts and emotions that he can recollect. Share the results of that experience (positive or negative), the insights that he gained, and how the children and/or wife can benefit from them.

DATE ATTEMPTED: _____

RESULTS: _____

_____

_____

_____

Project Two ☐ Same as Project One, except have mother share.

DATE ATTEMPTED: _____

RESULTS: _____

_____

_____

_____

22

The Spiritual/Devotional Life of the Home

SCRIPTURE READING: *Deuteronomy 6:4-9*

WHAT IS THE FOUNDATION OF A GOOD DEVOTIONAL LIFE?

The foundation of a good devotional life is the personal commitment of the parents to live a life that is Christian. If Christ is not real in the parents, they will never be able to make Him real to their children. Christ must be the center of the home. The home must be a place where the principles of the kingdom operate. This means that every Christian home should be characterized by:

• Many things which are not found there. A Christian home has the peculiar absence of many things that are central to the homes of the ungodly.

• The exaltation of Christian duties. There are many actions that are basic to the Christian life that need to be found in abundance in the home. Do we see expressions of the following in our homes?

- Loving one/another *(I John 4:7)*
- Esteeming one another better than ourselves *(Philippians 2:3)*
- Looking out for the interests of one another *(Philippians 2:4)*
- Setting one's affections on the things above *(Colossians 3:2)*
- Bearing one another's burdens *(Galatians 6:2)*
- Feeding one's enemies *(Romans 12:20)*
- Running the race of life with patience *(Hebrews 12:1)*
- Being kind to one another *(Ephesians 4:2)*

• The demonstration of the fruit of the Spirit *(Galatians 5:22-23)*. The home should be the first place where these virtues are expressed.

• The absence of the works of the flesh *(Galatians 5:17-21)*. There should be an absence of selfishness, covetousness, pride, and disregard for others' rights. These things which are so prevalent in the world have no place in the Christian home.

Christianity must be a real and spontaneous lifestyle in the home. When it is, the rewards are tremendous. If Christianity is not a way of life in the home, the children will be trained to be hypocritical *(Matthew 23:1-39; Romans 2:21-24)*.

WHAT DOES THE WORD "DEVOTIONS" MEAN?

The word "devotions" comes from words like "devote, devoted, devotee, devotion". The *Brittanica World Language Dictionary* says that:

DEVOTE means:

- To give or apply (attention, time, or oneself) completely to some activity, purpose, etc.
- To set apart; dedicate; consecrate

DEVOTED means:

- A feeling or a showing of devotion; ardent; zealous; devout
- Set apart, as by a vow, consecrated

DEVOTEE means:

- One zealously devoted, especially to religious observances; a zealot

DEVOTION means:

- The state of being devoted, as to religious faith or duty; zeal
- Strong attachment or affection expressing itself in earnest service.

Every Christian home is to be a place where we give or apply ourselves to the purposes of God, setting ourselves apart to the service of the Lord and the exaltation of His kingdom.

WHOSE RESPONSIBILITY IS IT FOR A GOOD DEVOTIONAL LIFE?

It is the father's responsibility. God has placed the father as the spiritual head of the home *(Ephesians 5:22; I Corinthians 11:3)*. As such, the charge of God is upon him to see that his children follow and respond to the ways of God *(Ephesisan 6:4)*. Every man from Adam to the present has been given this charge and every husband has been given a helpmeet to assist him. The initiative, however, does not belong to the wife, it belongs to the father. The father is the one who will be held accountable *(I Samuel 3:11-14; Exodus 4:24-26; Genesis 18:19)* Fathers must realize that since they are called of God, God will also equip them for this service. A college degree is not required, only a personal heart of devotion to t he Lord and a willingness to prepare.

WHAT ARE SOME GUIDELINES TO HELP FATHERS LEAD HOME DEVOTIONS?

- The father must be the initiator of spiritual enrichment in the home.

- The father must make sure that the atmosphere in the home is conducive to spiritual growth.

- The father must be *diligent* to pursue the spiritual well-being of family members.

- The father must continually encourage his children in leadership development.

- The father must make a time for special spiritual activities.

- The father must include everyone regardless of age.

- The father must be creative with devotional activities and avoid getting into a rut. The father should use the following ideas with variety:
  - Conversational prayer
  - Memorization of Scripture
  - Story-telling
  - Dramatization
  - Singing
  - Sharing
  - Praying for the sick
  - Devotional reading
  - Worship
  - Playing instruments
  - Bible reading
  - Composing songs
  - Testimonies
  - etc.

- The father must use every opportunity and happening in the home as a learning experience.

- The father must seek to answer the questions of the children correctly (even if it involves research).

- The father must be a feeder who is sensitive to the individual needs of his children.

- The father must be sensitive to the work of the Holy Spirit in the lives of his children.

- The father must be prepared to lead his child to the Lord.

- The father should not be afraid to include visitors in family exercises.

- The father must be willing to seek council and advice from other fathers.

- The father must continually encourage a trust, reliance, and acknowledgement of the Lord in all circumstances.

- The father should help to assure that the children retire to bed with the good things of the Lord on their hearts and minds.

WHAT ARE THE BENEFITS OF A GOOD DEVOTIONAL LIFE?

A good devotional life where the family seeks the Lord together can only bring forth good fruit.

- It establishes good devotional habits in the lives of the children.

- It demonstrates the fact that we recognize God as the head of the home.

- It draws the family closer together.

- It provides an opportunity to heal spiritual problems.

• It helps maintain good lines of communication between family members.

• It establishes the father as the spiritual leader of the home.

• It provides a context in which children can learn to know God, pray, and become familiar with Biblical truths.

• It produces love, joy, and peace in the home.

FAMILY PROJECTS

SECTION 3
LESSON 22
"The Spiritual/Devotional Life of the Home"

"And these words which I command thee this day, shall be in thine heart: And thou shalt teach them diligently unto thy children and shalt talk of them when thou sittest in thine house, and when thou walkest by the way; and when thou liest down, and when thou risest up"
(Deuteronomy 6:6,7).

Project One ☐
Have a family discussion, asking each member of the family to evaluate the present spiritual life of the home and state how they feel it could be improved.

DATE ATTEMPTED: _____

RESULTS: _____

_____

_____

Project Two ☐
For the next few days, let each member of the family be in charge of a 15-minute devotional time where they can lead the family until each person has had an opportunity.

DATE ATTEMPTED: _____

RESULTS: _____

_____

_____

Project Three ☐
In a family discussion, ask the question "What hinders us the most from having successful times of spiritual activity?" Make it a family project to work through these difficulties.

DATE ATTEMPTED: _____

RESULTS: _____

_____

Coordinating Family Activities

SCRIPTURE READING: Luke 2:39-52; Ecclesiastes 3:1-8

As a family increases, the children grow older and more demands are put upon the family schedule. It becomes increasingly important that all the activities of the family be properly coordinated in order to maintain peace and love in the home.

WHY IS IT IMPORTANT TO COORDINATE THE ACTIVITIES OF THE FAMILY?

Because of the many demands upon the family that increase as the family grows:

- Jobs
- Money
- Home
- Hospitality
- Teenagers
- Church activities
- Recreation
- Social Life
- Ministries
- School, education
- Responsibilities
- Priorities

Because of the danger of defeating the purpose of the family:

The home is to be the place of training the children, bringing them to maturity, building relationships, and developing Christ-like character. Too many activities and conflicts in scheduling can hinder these purposes.

Because of the danger of spoiling the atmosphere of the home:

The home should be a refuge from pressure and people, a place of peace, harmony, and love. Uncontrolled activity or disorganized schedules can breed strife and pressure and spoil this precious environment.

WHAT ARE THE RESULTS OF NOT ORGANIZING FAMILY ACTIVITIES?

Fragmented Family Life

If the members of a family are involved in too many activities, going too many different ways, it can quickly destroy the natural flow of family life and ruin the overall purpose of that family.

Unnecessary Pressure

An improper handling of the activities of the family

members can bring to bear pressures upon a home that were never meant to be and can be avoided.

Family Strife

Conflicts in scheduling and interests and time can create many a family feud. The pressures produced can turn into expressions of anger, frustration, jealousy, and even hatred.

Loss of Vision

It is easy to lose sight of God's purpose when we are too busy to consider, listen or look. The main purposes of the home can quickly be buried under layers of "activity".

WHO SHOULD COORDINATE FAMILY ACTIVITIES?

Both of the parents in a home are to fulfill this responsibility. Both of them have a unique role in coordinating family activities.

• The Father's Role: It is the father's ultimate responsibility, as the head of the home, to see to it that all things are properly coordinated, proper priorities are maintained, and things communicated around the home. A husband and father must discuss these things with his wife first, and then also the children.

• The Mother's Role: The mother can play the key role in coordinating all family activities because of her predominant role in the household responsibilities. The following are some helpful guidelines for the mother in planning out the family's activities.

–First, check with your husband (Colossians 3:18).
   Check his calendar and find out his plans appointments and desires.

–Discuss with your husband the children's activities and desires. Make him aware of what is going on. Make certain that he has all the facts.

–Be aware constantly of the children's activities. Keep on top of what they are doing and thinking. Find out ahead of time.

–Allow time for total family discussions. At least once a week, perhaps around a meal, find out everyone's feelings and plans.

WHAT ARE SOME OF THE MOST COMMON FRUSTRATIONS IN COORDINATING FAMILY ACTIVITIES, AND HOW SHOULD THEY BE HANDLED?

The following are some priority areas that are vital to family harmony in coordinating family activities. Listed with them are some questions that can be helpful in evaluating how successful your family is in each area.

MEALS

• Are you planning meals ahead?
• Are you attempting to maintain a consistent meal schedule?
• Are you flexible to rearrange meals depending on activities?
• Are you allowing enough time for meaningful fellowship during meals?

SLEEP

• Are your children getting enough sleep?
• Are you as a parent getting enough sleep?
• Should an activity be eliminated because of a lack of rest?
• Can you rearrange your schedule for more sleep when plans change?

DEVOTIONS

• Are you making the necessary sacrifices in order to have a meaningful family devotional time?
• Are you attempting to maintain a consistent time even during changes in plans?
• Are you trying to do too much or make devotions too lengthy?

FINANCES

• Are all members of the family aware of what is financially practical and what is not?
• Is this certain activity necessary?
• Can you afford this certain activity?
• Are there other alternatives you have not considered for financing this activity?

CHURCH SERVICES

• Are gatherings at church with other believers a priority in your home?
• Do you see the importance and benefit of consistent faithfulness to the meetings?
• Are you demonstrating and teaching Biblical priorities by faithfulness and punctuality to the church services?
• Is it expected of the children to attend all services together as a family?

FREE TIME

• Do family activities have priority for free time?
• Are free times planned out?
• Is everyone's desire considered as to how to use free time?

EMPLOYMENT

• Are you as a father, applying yourself with diligence to your job?
• Are you avoiding work on Sundays so as to set proper priorities and attend the House of God?
• Are you helping your teenagers set priorities and put part-time work in perspective?
• Does your employment consistently interfere with necessary family activities?

CHILDREN'S ACTIVITIES

- Are you as a parent supporting your child and encouraging him by attending his activities?
- Are you evaluating the place and importance of your children's activities?
- Are you being notified well ahead of time as to the upcoming activities of your children?

TRANSPORTATION

- Is car-pooling possible?
- Could someone else provide a ride for you or your children?
- Are your teens trained to drive safely? Are they given fair use of the car?
- Do you need a second vehicle?

EMERGENCIES AND UNEXPECTED ACTIVITIES

- Are you flexible enough to make last minute changes in your schedule?

FAMILY PROJECTS

SECTION 3
LESSON 23
"Coordinating Family Activities"

"And these words which I command thee this day, shall be in thine heart: And thou shalt teach them diligently unto thy children and shalt talk of them when thou sittest in thine house, and when thou walkest by the way; and when thou liest down, and when thou risest up"
(Deuteronomy 6:6,7).

Project One ☐

As a family project, design a family communication center with a bulletin board or blackboard for messages and a place to hang the family calendar.

DATE ATTEMPTED: _____

RESULTS: _____

_____

_____

Project Two ☐

Start a weekly habit to:
- Have a husband-wife discussion of activities.
- Have a family discussion time to talk about upcoming activities.

DATE ATTEMPTED: _____

RESULTS: _____

_____

_____

Project Three ☐

As a family, discuss priorities and balance in relation to how your family's activities are coordinated. Talk about everyone's responsibility to cooperate.

DATE ATTEMPTED: _____

RESULTS: _____

_____

_____

SECTION IV – THE ENTIRE FAMILY TOGETHER

Family Intimacy

SCRIPTURE READING: Ephesians 5:1-6,4; Hebrews 13:16; Song of Solomon

One of the most visible attacks of Satan in our day is the attack upon the family. In order for Satan to be successful, he must attack the very things that bind people together in bonds of love and commitment, that enable them to weather the storms of life, and come out on the other side even more closely united. His ferocious and all out attack centers on the spirit of family life. When the spirit of family togetherness is gone, it is only a matter of time before the form of family structure dissolves. Every wise Christian family should see the need for deepening and strengthening family ties.

The pattern for all human relationships is clearly seen in God's relationship to us. He desires a close and intimate relationship with us. The entire book of the Song of Solomon underscores this principle. Each member of the family must sense that he is intimately related to every other member. As each member is filled with this awareness, there is the free exchange of ideas, the mutual sharing of experiences, and the strengthening fellowship of family love. Since God has created in every individual the deep desire for intimate relationships, family life should be structured so as to satisfy this desire in every family member *(cf. Psalms 42:63).*

WHAT ARE SOME HINDRANCES TO HAVING THE SPIRIT OF TOGETHERNESS IN THE FAMILY?

• One hindrance is having too many individual activities which eliminate any time and opportunity for total family activity. Parents or children can unwittingly hinder family unity by not sacrificing their own individual schedule for the sake of family time.

• Not communicating regularly is another impediment. Daily communication about daily activities, reflecting opinions, desires and responses in open conversations are all necessary for togetherness.

• Another obstacle to family togetherness is not scheduling time for family togetherness.

• Furthermore, not resolving differences that arise will hinder family spirit. Unresolved conflicts grow into walls of resentment, hurt, or bitterness that isolate one family member from another.

• Too many *family* activities that result in a lot of activity but not much heart-to-heart, face-to-face, eye-to-eye relating will also hurt.

• Abusive, critical, or inflammatory speech that does not welcome a person into another's life but holds him at a distance, will also hinder family spirit.

• Physical violence destroys any inclination to share the deepest essence of soul and spirit. There can be no social intimacy in an atmosphere of violence or anger. It locks openness out and moves others to converse on half-truths, suspicion, fear, and apprehension, which are all self-protecting, not self-giving.

• Finally, not giving the family unit its due place of respect and importance will impede the family. By refusing to be open and honestly discuss even painful issues, the powerful message, "I don't care" is transmitted to the other members of the family.

WHAT DOES FAMILY INTIMACY REQUIRE?

The three basic ingredients to family intimacy are:

• Time
• Words
• Actions

TIME:

Both quantity of time and quality of time are important here. Not much quality can be packed into 30 seconds. Neither is there in two hours of television a great deal of quality. Those two hours may be acceptable programming, but very little communication takes place between family members. There must be *enough* time to converse, laugh, tell stories, relate incidents, share problems, and pray together. This type of time does not always automatically occur by itself. It must be pre-set by virtue of an ordered, scheduled life.

WORDS:

The words shared by family members either contribute to a binding, intimate relationship or contribute to isolationism *(Ephesians 4:29-32)*. Mom and Dad sharing words of love and encouragement in tender tones with each other and the children promotes a positive, open, and caring response in the entire family. How long has it been since you told each member of your family that you loved them?

ACTIONS:

The primary focus of actions in relationships is to confirm the positive Christian love and commitment that has been verbalized. It is easy for any member to go through the routine of family responsibilities without really expressing the love and concern for other members that needs to be there. Serving each other instead of waiting to be served carries the powerful message, "I care more for you than for myself". Those little things that take time to think of and do on a daily

basis go much further in deepending relationships than a once-a-year Christmas present. Because the disciples became faithful as servants, Jesus finally called them his friends.

WHO BEARS RESPONSIBILITY FOR DEVELOPING AND MAINTAINING THE SPIRIT OF FAMILY LIFE?

THE FATHER:

Just as our heavenly Father initiated and continues to initiate relationship with His children, so should the earthly father. Dad should be scheduling time, directing family activities, praying with each member, and opening up dialogues with any on any issue or problem that is brewing.

THE MOTHER:

Mothers have a special sixth sense that enables them to be the bearer of many burdens that often don't get brought up in the flow of daily activities. This special "radar" picks up the winds of adversity or difficulty before they become hurricanes. She deals with what is uncovered as well as makes her husband aware of special needs in the varying times and seasons in the lives of family members.

THE CHILDREN:

Children are taught to become servants to others by being taught to serve other family members. They also bear responsibility to share what is on their minds regardless of whether it seems to be positive or not. Parents promote this kind of openness and rapport through constant communication and enquiry. As the children grow older in such an atmosphere, they will only continue to hold dear what the family has meant to them by being willing to sacrifice their own individual schedule for family life.

WHAT ARE SOME HELPFUL HINTS FOR BUILDING FAMILY INTIMACY?

• Respond to each member of the family with personal attention whenever they speak.

• Set aside time for Mom and Dad to spend time alone together to share their concerns, interests, and failures.

• Schedule individualized activity occasionally so that each parent can spend some time alone with each child eg. shopping together, hunting trips, sports activity, attending some function, or going out to lunch together.

• Institute the family conference table for the discussion of decisions and problem-solving. Establish rules for communicating during this time. This should occur on a regular basis as well as when needs spontaneously occur.

• Have earnest family prayer for each other as well as for serious needs that arise.

• Have a constant stream of conversation between Mom and Dad and between parents and children. This keeps everyone "up-to-date" and informed.

• Give continual commendation, praise, and encouragement to each family member.

• Make the effort to communicate in crisis times. These are times of desperate need when the one in crisis needs to know that everyone still loves them.

• Establish family traditions that children and parents can look foward to for years to come.

• Have total family involvement in vacation planning.

• Have total family projects such as gardening, working in the yard, putting together jigsaw puzzles, picnicking, camping, etc.

• Eat as many meals together as possible.

• Do special things for members of the family when there is no special occasion.

• Place priority for the entire family on any functions with other relatives.

• Seek qualified counsel for any unresolved differences.

FAMILY • PROJECTS •

SECTION 4
LESSON 24
"Family Intimacy"

"And these words which I command thee this day, shall be in thine heart: And thou shalt teach them diligently unto thy children and shalt talk of them when thou sittest in thine house, and when thou walkest by the way; and when thou liest down, and when thou risest up"
(Deuteronomy 6:6,7).

Project One

☐ Dad and Mom discuss what things hinder the development and growth of family life, openly and honestly making the needed adjustments and additions. With teenage children, this can be a discussion in which they are included.

DATE ATTEMPTED: _____

RESULTS: _____

_____

_____

Project Two

☐ Have a time of sharing in the family in which each member shares what he appreciates the most about all of the other individual members.

DATE ATTEMPTED: _____

RESULTS: _____

_____

_____

Project Three

☐ For families with older children, purchase or borrow the UNGAME and play it on a family night. This game promotes the sharing of opinions, desires, and aspirations. It is an easy, fun-filled, and unique way of finding out how and what family members think.

DATE ATTEMPTED: _____

RESULTS: _____

_____

_____

25

The Relationship Between the Home and the Church

SCRIPTURE READING: Acts 2:42-47

Often times in church, people have a difficult time establishing priorities in their activities because they do not understand the relationship of the Church to the home. In the New Testament it is very clear that the home was very important in the life of the early Church *(Acts 2:44-47)*. The teachings received in the temple were to be worked out in the home on a day-to-day basis.

HOW DO THE CHURCH AND THE HOME SUPPORT EACH OTHER?

God wants both the Church and the home to be strong and to support each other.

God wants the strengh of the home to support the Church, and He wants the strength of the Church to support the home.

WHICH IS MORE IMPORTANT, THE CHURCH OR THE HOME?

It must be remembered that every local church is made up of people who are also members of families.

- The pastor is a family member.
- The elders are family members.
- The deacons are family members.
- Every member of the body is a family member.

It must be remembered that the Church and the home are not meant to be in competition, ie, having their resources pitted against one another.

The dictionary defines competiton as:

- "Contention of two or more for the same object or for superiority; rivalry."
- "The independent endeavor of two or more persons to obtain the business patronage of a third by offering more advantageous terms."

It must be remembered that there will be possible points of tension between the Church and the home that could create a spihit of competition if not handled correctly. Some of the tension points include conflicts over:

- Scheduling
- Doctrine
- Authority
- Time commitments
- Church policies
- Church standards

It must be remembered that there must be a strong relationship between the home and the Church in order for God's purposes to be accomplished in both places. Noah's ark is a good example of the importance of the family and the Church relating to each other. Notice the following:

- The ark (a type of the Church) was necessary for the preservation of the family *(Hebrews 10:25)*.
- The building of the ark was a family project *(Genesis 6:1-10)*.
- The ark with the family in it was on display for seven days before the flood came *(Genesis 7:10)*. The home and the Church together are to display to the world the glory of God *(Isaiah 60:1-5)*.
- The ark with the family was a place of safety that was builded together to overcome in the days of storm in the end time.

Which was most important, the ARK or the FAMILY? Both!

HOW CAN PARENTS HELP TO KEEP THE HOME AND THE CHURCH IN PROPER PERSPECTIVE?

Recognize that God desires the Christian home to be totally identified with the purposes of God which are expressed and fulfilled through the Church. There is no evidence in the New Testament that any believer enjoyed the experience and benefits of salvation who was not vitally connected to the Church of the Lord Jesus Christ.

Realize the importance of endeavoring to keep the unity of the Spirit in the bond of peace *(Ephesians 4:3)*. There must be a unity between the home and the Church if there is to be protection and preservation in the last days *(I Corinthians 1:10)*.

Be aware of the tactics that Satan will try to use to destroy the unity between the home and the Church.

- Lack of communication: There must be a constant effort to understand what is really being said. When misunderstandings arise they must not be promoted, but they should be resolved by communication between local leadership and the parents.

- Double vision: Satan will try to bring confusion by giving every member a different vision, making it double-minded and rendering it ineffective. Parents should be careful to support the corporate vision of the Church in their families and help inspire the faith of the next generation to do the same.

- Defaming leadership: When parents have "preacher for dinner" and in other ways challenge the direction of the Church leadership in front of their children, they are undermining the influence of the Church in the lives of their children and are ultimately giving their children an excuse for later rebellion.

Check negative attitudes before they become a problem. Many wrong attitudes develop around small things, such as:

- The number of Church services
- The number of Church activities
- The length of Church services
- The type of music that is played
- The decisions concerning the facilities or
- The building programs decisions concerning finances
- The particular emphasis of that local church
- The Sunday Sermons or preachers

Church leaders are aware that many people have different views on many different subjects. After considering all of the views, because they are leaders, they must take some positive action. Many of these areas are matters of judgement and taste and, hence, when a decision is made, invariably it does not totally please everyone. This happens very often in a home between parents and children. Perhaps God is giving us an opportunity to demonstrate before our children what it means to submit to those that are over you. Parents can be sure that their children will learn much about how to respond to parental authority by how their parents respond to Church authority.

Disrespect at home toward the Church will undermine the respect that the young of the flock should maintain. In their day of trouble, they will have no respect for those who might be able to help them. Mutual respect and support are necessary.

Communicate positive attitudes toward the Lord and His House.

- Parents should teach their children respect for the Lord's day.
- Parents should make the Church gatherings something to be desired.
- Parents should make the Church a priority in attendance.
- Parents should reinforce at home what is being said in Church.

As the days of evil and deception grow worse, the Church and the home must come closer together in oneness, cooperation, and respect. The salvation of our families will be secure as long as we relate our lives to each other in the Body of Christ *(II Timothy 3:1-17)*.

• F A M I L Y   P R O J E C T S •

SECTION 4
LESSON 25
"The Relationship Between the Home and the Church"

"And these words which I command thee this day, shall be in thine heart: And thou shalt teach them diligently unto thy children and shalt talk of them when thou sittest in thine house, and when thou walkest by the way; and when thou liest down, and when thou risest up"
(Deuteronomy 6:6,7).

Project One   ☐ Have your family spend a time of prayer together praying for the Church, its leadership, and its programs.

DATE ATTEMPTED: _____

RESULTS: _____

_____

_____

_____

Project Two   ☐ Discuss with your family the importance of each of the Church services and the need for them. If you have teenagers, emphasize the importance of adjusting activities and work schedules to give first place to God and His House.

DATE ATTEMPTED: _____

RESULTS: _____

_____

_____

_____

The Role of Grandparents in the Home

SCRIPTURE READING: Titus 2:1-15; I Timothy 5:1-8

One of the characteristics of a nation that is undergoing moral decay is the tendency to cast off the old and give them little or no respect *(Deuteronomy 28:50; Lamentations 5:12; Isaiah 47:6)*. One of the characteristics of this day is to cast off the old, with their counsel *(Psalm 71:9)*. The beautiful thing about our day is that God is calling both young and old together. In almost every home, God has given us, by means of grandparents, the opportunity to tap the wisdom of the old and teach our children to honor and respect the aged. Often, families fail to tap this wisdom for two reasons. First, older people have a wrong view of themselves and fail to take the initiative. Secondly, the parents often fail to give their parents the honor and respect that is due them.

WHAT IS TO BE AN OLDER PERSON'S ATTITUDE TOWARD OLD AGE?

- They are to look forward to old age.

- It is a reward for righteousness *(Deuteronomy 5:33; 11:21; I Kings 3:14; Psalms 91:16; Proverbs 3:2; 9:11; 10:27)*.

- It is a time to enjoy the fruit of one's hands *(Isaiah 65:22; Proverbs 17:6)*.

- It is to be a time of real fruitfulness *(Psalm 92:14)* and strength *(Job 5:26)*.

- They are to look at it as a blessing and not try to hide gray hairs. In Old Testament times, old age was greatly desired and its attainment was regarded as a divine blessing.

  - A gray head is a crown of glory *(Proverbs 16:31)*.
  - A gray head is the beauty of the aged *(Proverbs 20:29)*.

- They are to realize that God is very present and still working in their lives *(Isaiah 46:4)*.

WHAT DIVINE QUALITY IS POSSESSED BY THE AGED?

- Superior wisdom and understanding *(Job 12:12,20)* to the aged. Hence, in the Scriptures we always find them in positions of authority and guidance.

• "Much experience is the crown of old men, and the fear of God is their glory" *(Ecclesiaties 25:6).*

• It should be noted that it is possible to waste your life in folly and not acquire the wisdom that normally comes with years *(Ecclesiasties 4:13; Job 32:9).*

WHAT IS THE MINISTRY OF THE OLDER TO THE YOUNGER?

• The older are to be people of counsel *(Ezekiel 7:26).*

• It is wisdom for the young to seek their counsel and give heed to it *(Exodus 18:1; 13-27).*

• It is folly for the young to reject the counsel of the older *(Rehoboam: I Kings 12:1-5; II Chronicles 10:1-13).*

• The older are to guide the younger generation into the purposes of God.

  • God reveals His plans through the elders of Israel *(Exodus 3:16-18; 12:21; 17:5-6).*
  • The elders were responsible to teach and stabilize the younger generation *(Deuteronomy 32:7; Job 32:7; Joel 1:2; Titus 2:2-5).*
  • The older are to impart their wisdom and experience to the young that they might be able to enter in *(Psalm 71:18).*
  • The older are to lead the way when God says build *(Ezra 5:1-5,9).*
  • God holds the older responsible in a good measure for what happens *(Isaiah 3:14; 9:13-17).*

• The older are to be examples to the younger (I Samuel 12:1-5; II Timothy 1:5)

WHAT SHOULD BE THE ATTITUDE OF THE YOUNG TO THE OLD?

• They should honor and respect the older *(Leviticus 19:32).*

  • The men who are elders are honorable in God's eyes *(Isaiah 9:14-15).*
  • They are the spiritual fathers and mothers in the House of the Lord *(Matthew 19:29),* and they should have the same respect *(Proverbs 23:22; Exodus 20:12).*
  • To show lack of respect to the elders will bring judgement *(II Kings 2:23,24; Deuteronomy 27:16; Proverbs 20:20; 30:17; Matthew 15:4-6).*

• They should seek out and listen to their counsel *(Proverbs 1:8-9; Ephesians 6:1-3).*

• They should be cautious about their own opinions in the presence of the elder *(Job 32:4-7; I Timothy 5:1).*

• They should follow the faith of the old to be strong *(Hebrews 13:7; Philippians 4:9; 3:17).*

• They should not cast off the old *(Psalms 71:9).*

WHAT ARE SOME WAYS THAT PARENTS CAN HELP THEIR CHILDREN APPRECIATE THEIR GRANDPARENTS?

• Parents should visit their parents often to maintain a vital relationship with them.

• Parents should always treat their parents with respect, honor, and dignity.

• Parents should seek the counsel of their parents.

• Parents should emphasize the positive qualities in the lives of their parents to their children.

• Parents should encourage their children to do special things for the grandparents.

• Parents should make sure their children spend time with their grandparents.

• Parents should be prepared to assist their parents when they are old.

• Parents should not take advantage of grandparents in expecting them to be their regular babysitters.

WHAT ARE SOME WAYS THAT GRANDPARENTS CAN BECOME MORE INVOLVED IN THE LIVES OF THEIR GRANDCHILDREN?

When considering this area, a key word is "availability". Because most often in our society grandparents live apart from their sons and daughters and their grandchildren, they must make themselves available as often as they can in their particular situation. Grandchildren should grow up relating naturally to their grandparents.

The following are only a few suggestions for ways in which grandparents can naturally include the grandchildren in their lives.

• Assist the parents, if possible, when the new grandchildren arrive.

• Visit at times on your own initiative. During these times take an active involvement with the children.

  • Holding them
  • Feeding them
  • Rocking them
  • Putting them to bed
  • Telling them a story
  • Playing with them
  • Praying with them
  • Talking with them

• Take pictures of the children and pictures of you with the children. These pictures could be put into an album and could be used to shape many wonderful memories.

• Take the grandchildren with you on trips, on outings, to the park, or even shopping.

• Include your grandchildren in the everyday duties of life. Have them help you with yard work, washing the car, cleaning the garage, etc.

• Involve the older children in your prayer life. Let them know this is a priority in your lives.

• Let them spend a Sunday afternoon with you occasionally.

• Be willing to help the grandchildren with homework when you are aware of it.

• Tell the grandchildren stories of your day. Show them pictures of a generation ago to help broaden their thinking and world view.

• Help teach the grandchildren to work with their hands by sharing crafts and skills (sewing, knitting, woodworking, drawing, painting, etc.) with them.

• If a grandparent has a real special activity like fishing, hunting, hiking, etc., why not take the grandchild with him? These activities will build happy memories in the mind of the child.

• Help your grandchild with a special project.

Of course, all of these suggestions are based on certain ideal conditions. There are many variables that can affect how much of these kind of things can be done. The age, health, and geographical location of the grandparents may make many of these things impossible. However, there is something every grandparent can do, even if it is simply an occasional telephone call, or letter. All will contribute to building happy memories for all.

FAMILY · PROJECTS ·

SECTION 5
LESSON 26
"The Role of Grandparents in the Home"

"And these words which I command thee this day, shall be in thine heart: And thou shalt teach them diligently unto thy children and shalt talk of them when thou sittest in thine house, and when thou walkest by the way; and when thou liest down, and when thou risest up"
(Deuteronomy 6:6,7).

Project One ☐ Invite the grandparents over to a special evening of honor. Prepare special questions for them to answer in the presence of the children. Take notes on principles that you glean from their answers.

DATE ATTEMPTED: _____

RESULTS: _____

_____

Project Two ☐ If you are a grandparent, plan a special outing where you can share some quality time alone with your grandchildren.

DATE ATTEMPTED: _____

RESULTS: _____

Project Three ☐ Spend one evening with your children discussing the questions: Why can we be thankful for grandparents? How can we show them our thankfulness? Spend some time making a special card or present for the grandparents which expresses your love to them.

DATE ATTEMPTED: _____

RESULTS: _____

Project Four

☐ If you are a grandparent, plan specific ways in which you can help to impart one of your skills to your grandchildren.

DATE ATTEMPTED: _____

RESULTS: _____

_____

Relating to Relatives

SCRIPTURE READING: Galatians 6:10; Ephesians 3:15; Romans 12:18; I Timothy 5:4,8

The definition of a relative is: belonging to or connected with; a person connected by kinship or blood relationship. In these days of restoration, as God moves to restore family relationships *(Malachi 4:6),* special attention must be given to the total family unit and how God intended it to function. It is just as much of a reproach for a spiritual fracture to separate parents, as it is for division and strife to separate relatives within a family. God intended that the total family unit, as many generations as are living, to unite together to form the backbone of society and the Church. The strength of family ties is a powerful source for perpetuating good or evil for several generations.

WHAT BIBLICAL PRINCIPLES GOVERN RELATIONSHIPS TO RELATIVES?

CHRISTIAN RELATIVES

Any relatives that are genuine born-again believers should be treated like any non-relatives who are members of the Body of Christ. *Galatians 6:10* says "... especially those of the household of faith". They should be received as brothers or sisters in Christ, not as some unique third category of individuals.

NON-CHRISTIAN RELATIVES

Any relatives who are not genuine born-again believers are also to be treated in a Biblical manner:

- "Do good unto all men ..." *(Galatians 6:10)*
- "Live peaceably with all men ..." *(Romans 12:18)*
- Be willing to give to meet their needs *(I Timothy 5:8)*

HOW CAN I NOT FELLOWSHIP WITH THE UNFRUITFUL WORKS OF DARKNESS AND YET MAINTAIN FAMILY TIES?

The answer lies in the true meaning of the word fellowship. Jesus had a great deal of close involvement with the unsaved, but never did He have fellowship with them. The word fellowship means "to share something in common with another". The Christian has *nothing* in common with the unbeliever, thus, his basis of relationship to his unsaved relatives is one focused on a witness of Christ. Everything he says, does, and is, should point to the superior lifestyle he possesses, not in a deliberate effort to condemn, but in a positive effort to make the unbelieving relative curious, hungry, and finally a seeker of what he possesses. This effort must be carried out with great carefulness, consideration, and Holy Spirit guidance.

WHAT UNIQUE DIFFICULTIES ARE ENCOUNTERED IN RELATING TO RELATIVES?

- Knowing how to meet seemingly impossible expectations

- Knowing when to offer advice and when to withold it

- Knowing when to offer assistance of any kind and when to refrain from offering assistance

- Knowing how to divide family wealth in leaving a will

- Knowing how much time to devote to activities with relatives

- Knowing how to respond to well-intentioned but unwanted in-laws' advice

All of these difficulties can be solved by clear and forthright communication. Making one's motives clear is the most important element of communication between relatives. Since relatives often are suspicious of one another's motives, establishing a track record of good motives is vitally necessary. Any misunderstandings or offenses that occur should be handled right away in a Biblical manner *(Matthew 18:15-22* and *Ephesians 4:24-32).*

WHAT ARE SOME GENERAL GUIDELINES FOR MAINTAINING GOOD RELATIONSHIPS WITH RELATIVES?

- Keep up regular contact with them.

- Make extra special efforts to communicate clearly your desires and intentions.

- Express obviously and frequently your appreciation for them and anything they have done on your behalf.

- Pray for your relatives.

- Pray for wisdom in relating to your relatives.

- Take the initiative to clear up any misunderstandings that arise.

- Don't presume on their generosity or ability to accept graciously your blunders.

- For serious matters of counsel, recommend they seek qualified spiritual help (nothing will hurt relations more than a counseling error on your part — or something they see as an error on your part).

- Be hospitable, kind, and tolerant of unsaved relatives. Don't require them to be pharisaical around you.

- Be willing to sacrifice your immediate family schedule to accommodate activities with other relatives.

- Be on the lookout to catch sight of needs that you might be able to meet. Meet them without waiting for thanks.

- Pay back any debts owing to relatives as quickly as agreed upon.

- Don't keep records of how much you have done versus how much they have done. True love has an inexhaustible supply.

WHAT BIBLICAL PRINCIPLES GOVERN THE PLACE OF IN-LAWS IN FAMILY RELATIONSHIPS?

- *Genesis 2:24* speaks of a kind of leaving that occurs between parents and child in order to form a new family unit.

- *Ephesians 6:1,2* enjoins children to honor father and mother. This commandment is without time duration.

The leaving that occurs on the part of the daughter and son who plan to wed is a leaving that severs the umbilical cord of emotional, financial, spiritual, and social dependence upon their respective parents. They now come into a relationship with each other as man and wife in which they together become totally responsible for their own life together. Both of their entire resources must now be given to shaping their own family life. Any relationship with parents that siphons off those resources or tries to prevent the two of them from failing in some area, only delays what must inevitably occur: the two newly-weds standing on their own, building a relationship together of strength, stability, and responsible living.

To release adult children to this adventure in life in no way conveys a message of lack of love on the part of the parents. To the contrary, it expresses confidence in them which they so desperately need.

The relationship of love and honor between parents and adult children must still be maintained by the newly-weds as they are graciously appreciative of how their parents have prepared them to walk through life responsibly and Biblically.

Advice and counsel on the part of the parents is now given on the basis of request by the new family, not on the basis of need. Wise children will still seek advice and respond to the good advice of their parents or in-laws as Moses took the wise counsel of his father-in-law that probably saved his life and health *(Exodus 18:6-26).*

WHAT BENEFITS ARE AFFORDED THOSE WHO DEVELOP AND MAINTAIN GOOD RELATIONSHIPS WITH RELATIVES?

- Aid in time of trouble or need

- The witness of Christianity to the unsaved within the family as well as those outside the family

- The strengthening of family identity and the sense of belonging

- A resource of wisdom, strength, and counsel

- A unique type of lifelong friendship that adds a dimension of fulfilment to life

- A life-picture of the beauty that should characterize the family of God

FAMILY PROJECTS •

SECTION 5
LESSON 27
"Relating to Relatives"

"And these words which I command thee this day, shall be in thine heart: And thou shalt teach them diligently unto thy children and shalt talk of them when thou sittest in thine house, and when thou walkest by the way; and when thou liest down, and when thou risest up"
(Deuteronomy 6:6,7).

Project One
☐ Father leads in family discussion naming each of the relatives, giving a reason for his appreciation of each one and then allowing the rest of the family to make their contribution.

DATE ATTEMPTED: _____

RESULTS: _____

_____

_____

Project Two
☐ Have a time of special prayer just for relatives, listing each one and praying for special needs, encouraging each member to be involved in the prayer.

DATE ATTEMPTED: _____

RESULTS: _____

_____

_____

Project Three
☐ If possible, plan a family outing with some relatives you haven't seen for a while.

DATE ATTEMPTED: _____

RESULTS: _____

_____

_____

SECTION V — SPECIAL RELATIONSHIPS IN THE FAMILY

Teenagers in the Home

SCRIPTURE READING: Ecclesiastes 11:9-12:1, I Timothy 4:12

The time when children enter in to the teen years (13-19) is generally referred to as adolescence and is a time of change and growth. Many parents, facing this period for the first time with their oldest child, discover unique and different challenges for themselves as well as their teenager. It is wise to examine some basic principles that will help both parents and teens go through this time with confidence and success.

IS ADOLESCENCE DIFFERENT THAN OTHER TIMES OF LIFE?

Yes — most definitely! Adolescence (the teenage years) can best be described as a transition between childhood and audlthood. A teenager could be called an "in-between-ager".

It is during this time that a young person can no longer be considered a child and yet has by no means reached the level of being considered an adult. It is a difficult stage of being in-between childhood and adulthood. Because of the unique problems of this age, it is wise for us to take special care in seeking God's unique solutions.

DOES THE BIBLE GIVE ANY INSTRUCTIONS SPECIFICALLY FOR TEENAGERS OR THEIR PARENTS?

Interestingly enough, there are many stories of young people in the Bible and many principles that relate to their specific problems.

Biblical examples of young people God used:

- Joseph *(Genesis 37:2*
- Samuel *(I Samuel 1,2)*
- David *(I Samuel 16,17)*
- Solomon *(I Kings 3:5-13)*

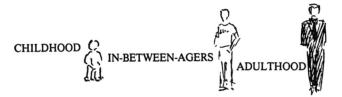

CHILDHOOD   IN-BETWEEN-AGERS   ADULTHOOD

- Josiah *(II Chronicles 34:1-3)*
- Jeremiah *(Jeremiah 1:4-9)*
- Uzziah *(II Chronicles 26:1-5)*
- Jesus *(Luke 2:40-52)*

God has specific purposes for young people:

- To use them while they are young *(Lamentations 3:27; Ecclesiastes 12:1).*
- To train and prepare them for future use *(Malachi 4:6; I John 2:14).*
- To make them examples of faith in their youth *(I Timothy 4:12).*
- To help them enjoy the time of their youth *(Ecclesiastes 11:9,10).* True joy and happiness come by living within the framework and guidelines of God's Word *(Proverbs 29:18).*

WHAT PROBLEMS ARE UNIQUE TO THE TEENAGE TIME OF LIFE?

- Teenagers are experiencing physical, mental, emotional, and social changes never before experienced.

  - Physical and mental development
  - Awakening sexual desires
  - Increased peer group pressure

- Teens are coming to terms with their self-identity — finding out who they are.

- Young people are learning greater levels of responsibility, beginning the process of facing real life.

  - Working at a job
  - Handling finances
  - Driving a car
  - Using their time
  - Bearing responsibility

- Youth begin dating the opposite sex with lifetime consequences facing them, determined by their standards and moral guidelines.

- Goals for the future are now examined more closely because of the imminent need for life direction.

  - Educational goals
  - Vocational goals
  - Financial goals
  - Spiritual goals

HOW SHOULD PARENTS RELATE TO THEIR CHILDREN AS TEENAGERS?

It is vitally important for parents to recognize the critical stage through which their children are now passing. Parents need to learn how to relate to their teenager in a different way than before. A teenager is an emerging adult and can no longer be treated as just a child. However, because childishness will still inevitably manifest itself, a parent needs to develop a balance of trust and authority that will produce a secure and happy "in-between-ager".

- This cannot always be a planned thing, but it must take place frequently. A top priority for parents of teens should be a sensitivity to the spirit of their child to know when a time of sharing and listening is necessary.

- These times of sharing should not necessarily be times of "preaching" or giving adult advice, as much as times of listening, understanding, caring and sharing — discussing difficulties in a way that demonstrates respect and trust in the young person.

- These discussion times should not always be based on a problem, or only take place when discipline is being applied. The reason most parents find themselves constantly disciplining their teenager is because they are not spending quality time in healthy, happy communication before the difficulties arise.

Parents must approach teenage discipline in a different way than childhood discipline.

- Teenagers are no longer children that can simply be told and spanked. They are emerging adults, and although they may be a long way from maturity, they do need to be approached differently than children in regard to correction and discipline.

- Although using the rod for correction is appropriate for children (and may be for some younger teenagers, depending on the situation) it should be viewed generally as inappropriate for adolescents (particularly older teens). Other forms of correction such as the removal of privileges, grounding, etc. should be used.

- Teenagers should clearly understand (and usually want to understand) why they are being disciplined. Time should be taken, without anger, to explain the offense, the Scriptural principles violated, and the reason for the necessary discipline.

- The following diagram illustrates the balance necessary when disciplining adolescents:

Teenagers must be disciplined in a balanced way using a combination of the following "child" and "adult" approaches:

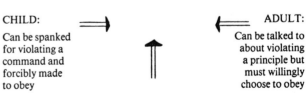

CHILD:
Can be spanked for violating a command and forcibly made to obey

ADULT:
Can be talked to about violating a principle but must willingly choose to obey

TEENAGER:
Can be disciplined for violating a command or a principle and made to obey along with an appeal to do it willingly.

Parents should help their young people develop responsibility.

Part of God's design for children is to go through a time of life in which they must learn to face personal responsibilities. This time of growing independence in the life of a teenager can either be a frustrating time of strife between parent and child or a time of recognized opportunity for the parents to train their child to be a mature, responsible adult.

- Parents initially begin to foster an attitude of responsibility in their teenage son or daughter by demonstrating an attitude of trust and slowly increasing their child's areas of responsibility. This gradually increases as the young person matures until one day, when leaving the home, he or she takes full responsibility for his own life and future.

- Parents can use many practical means to train their children to be responsible. The key for success is giving them as much trust and responsibility as they can handle depending upon their age and development. For example:
  - Household chores
  - Education — homework
  - Their first job
  - Handling money (budgeting, saving, tithing, giving, etc.)
  - Driving the car
  - Serving the church (workdays, volunteering labor, youth ministries)
  - Projects at home

WHAT ARE SOME SPECIFIC PROBLEMS THAT PARENTS MAY FACE WHEN RAISING TEENS AND HOW CAN THEY SOLVE THEM?

After having raised their children in a certain manner for 10-12 years, many parents run up against unique and difficult circumstances when their children enter adolescence. Parents find themselves in many similar problems and can find wisdom and help by sharing with other parents or counseling with a pastor, elder, or youth pastor.

The following are some common problem areas:

- Communication Breakdown — won't talk or open up
  - ☐ Your teenager may be experiencing some guilt, or may feel that you, as a parent, don't understand or won't listen.

- Stubborness — resisting authority
  - ☐ Recognize this as a common tendency and problem among teens. Don't over-react. You may need to spend more time in positive communication and listening to them.
  - ☐ If this attitude persists or develops into deeper rebellion, seek qualified Christian counsel.

- Moodiness — emotional changes and unpredictability
  - ☐ Many things may cause this, including physical problems, but, again, communication is essential, with love and understanding *(Proverbs 15:1)*. Find the source of the problem if possible.

- Peer Pressure — wanting to please friends more than parents
  - ☐ Although this, too, is a common tendency, it can be counteracted with a parent who will spend quality time with his/her teenager.

- Ungratefulness — taking things and people for granted
  - ☐ Privileges must always be balanced with responsibilities and ungrateful young people often are not carrying their share of the load. We value most what we have to work for most diligently.

- Moral failure — violating family standards
  - ☐ As a major temptation area for youth, many young people fall into the snare of the enemy here in different degrees. After a failure experience, parents must maintain great love and understanding, realistically facing this difficulty in a godly manner for the sake of present and future restoration.

It is encouraging and comforting for us to remember that God has promised a revival between parents and children in the last days. Let us believe to see our own homes restored to peace and harmony; avoiding the rebellion, hatred, and sinfulness of our generation, and to see our own children grow up to serve God with all their hearts *(Malachi 4:6; Luke 1:17; Psalm 144:12)*.

FAMILY • PROJECTS •

SECTION 5
LESSON 28
"Teenagers in the Home"

"And these words which I command thee this day, shall be in thine heart: And thou shalt teach them diligently unto thy children and shalt talk of them when thou sittest in thine house, and when thou walkest by the way; and when thou liest down, and when thou risest up"
(Deuteronomy 6:6,7).

Project One ☐ Have a special dinner out with just Mom, Dad and your teen and talk about communication and discipline.

DATE ATTEMPTED: _____

RESULTS: _____

_____

_____

Project Two ☐ If you have not done so already, plan a time with your teenager to write down goals for life, standards for dating, guidelines for jobs, principles for handling money, etc.

DATE ATTEMPTED: _____

RESULTS: _____

_____

_____

Project Three ☐ Call for an appointment with your youth pastor or elder and discuss the present relationship between you and your teenager.

DATE ATTEMPTED: _____

RESULTS: _____

_____

_____

God's View of Dating

SCRIPTURE READING: I Thessalonians 4:1-8; I Corinthians 6:9-20

As families grow and young people move through the teen years, new areas of concern arise. One of the most important is teaching children how to relate properly to other young people, particularly those of the opposite sex. It is crucial for parents and young people alike to know and understand God's principles for this important area.

WHY IS THE AREA OF PROPER DATING SO IMPORTANT?

- Because relationships with the opposite sex touch on one of the strongest physical drives of man.

  - Temptations will be strong to misuse or abuse these desires.
  - Self-control must be learned in order to bring about ultimate fulfilment.

- Because these relationships affect future generations and family happiness.

- Because when this area of dating is abused, the results can be devastating.

WHY ARE THERE PROBLEMS WITH DATING?

- Often parents and young people alike lack knowledge of God's principles for this crucial area *(Hosea 4:6)*.

- Because of the strong sexual desires related to this area — temptations abound *(I Peter 2:11; James 1:14-15)*.

- The society in which we live has perverted the godly concepts of pure relationships *(Acts 2:40; Philippians 2:15)*.

- Many conflicting voices have confused the clear issues of right and wrong and the meanings of words such as "dating", "romance", "love", etc. *(Isaiah 5:20)*.

SHOULD CHRISTIANS HAVE DIFFERENT DATING RELATIONSHIPS THAN THE WORLD?

Yes! Although it is easy for even Christians to fall into the ways of the world, God's Word gives clear instruction that all our relationships are to be unique, pure, and wholesome. God's ways are different than the world's ways, particularly in relation to dating and sexual relationships *(Proverbs 14:12; Jeremiah 21:8).*

GOD'S WAYS FOR DATING	WORLD'S WAYS FOR DATING
• God-centered relationships	• Self-centered relationships
• **BASIS:** Wholesome attraction, commitment to God, solid friendship	• **BASIS:** Natural attraction, feelings, sexual desires
• **GOAL:** Mutual spiritual edification	• **GOAL:** Self-centered gratification
• Giving attitude	• Receiving attitude
• Absolute moral standards	• No absolute moral standards
• Focus on spirit and soul	• Focus on body and soul
• Taking time to get to know each other	• Moving quickly to take advantage of each other
• Relationship inclusive of the Body of Christ	• Relationship exclusive and possessive
RESULTS:	**RESULTS:**
• Stronger relationship with God	• Weakened relationship with God
• Stronger relationships with others	• Weaker relationships with others
• Healthy self-image	• Unhealthy self-image
• Character development	• Character degeneration
• Greater motivation	• Draining of motivation
• Increased fulfillment	• Decreased fulfillment
• Good example to others	• Bad example to others
• Peace	• Confusion, strife, and pain
• Deep joy	• Emptiness and sorrow
• Abundant life in all areas	• Death (in all areas)

WHAT IS GOD'S VIEW OF THE WAY ROMANTIC RELATIONSHIPS SHOULD BE?

Romantic relationships should be guided by the absolute moral standards of God's Word.

THE SIN:	THE DEFINITION:
Idolatry	Exalting someone else above God
The Scriptures: I Corinthians 6:9,10; Colossians 3:5	
Lasciviousness	The stirring up of sensual desires
Ephesians 4:19; I Peter 4:3	
Defrauding	Using someone for self-gratification

I Thessalonians 4:3-6	
Concupiscence	Heavy physical involvement
Colossians 3:5; I Thessalonians 4:5; Romans 7:8	
Fornication	Sexual consummation outside of marriage
Galatians 5:19-21; I Corinthians 6:15-20	

Romantic desires are God-given and are meant to lead ultimately to marriage *(Proverbs 5:15-20).*

• These desires must be brought under the control of the Holy Spirit.
• These desires can only be consummated righteously in marriage.

God's Word encourages the development of sincere friendships and healthy relationships between the sexes.

- A sincere, wholesome friendship with the opposite sex is a good thing.
- Relationships with physical involvement or inappropriate verbal expressions of "love" prior to a lifetime commitment, undermine God's ultimate design.

Romantic relationships in the Body of Christ should be based upon brother and sister friendships not external beauty *(Proverbs 31:30)*.

- We are all "brothers and sisters" in Christ *(I Timothy 5:1,2)*

  - We are to trust one another with all purity.
  - We are to treat one another as members of the same family, the family of God.

  - Ask yourself, "How would I treat my own natural brother or sister?"

- We are to be "friends" of one another *(III John 14)* as we are with Jesus *(John 15:14,15)*.

- One always seeks the best interest of a friend *(Proverbs 17:17)*.
- One does not use a friend for selfish purposes *(John 15:13)*.

- We are to "fellowship" together *(Acts 2:42)*.

  - We should have many frequent activities together within the framework of the Christian community *(Hebrews 10:25)*.
  - Our fellowship should never be exclusive *(I John 1:7)*.

  - Our fellowship should help us relate to many different people in the church *(I Timothy 5:1-3)*.

- We are all "members of one another" in the Body of Christ *(Romans 12:5)*.

  - We should treat each other with honor and respect *(I Corinthians 12:24,25)*.
  - We are to work together to fulfil God's will on earth *(Galatians 6:2)*.

The following diagram illustrates how the people gradually reach marital commitment:

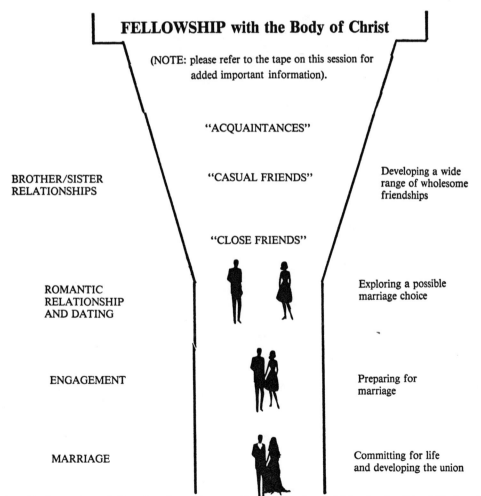

FELLOWSHIP with the Body of Christ

(NOTE: please refer to the tape on this session for added important information).

"ACQUAINTANCES"

BROTHER/SISTER RELATIONSHIPS

"CASUAL FRIENDS"

Developing a wide range of wholesome friendships

"CLOSE FRIENDS"

ROMANTIC RELATIONSHIP AND DATING

Exploring a possible marriage choice

ENGAGEMENT

Preparing for marriage

MARRIAGE

Committing for life and developing the union

Dating should always be solidly related to this overall context. Relationships that are exclusive, private, and imbalanced only detract from God's purposes and can seriously hurt all those involved.

God desires wholesome, balanced, relationships that develop within the family of God and reserves exclusive and imtimate romantic relationships for the time in young people's lives when they are ready to make a marriage commitment.

FAMILY • PROJECTS •

SECTION 5
LESSON 29
"God's View of Dating"

"And these words which I command thee this day, shall be in thine heart: And thou shalt teach them diligently unto thy children and shalt talk of them when thou sittest in thine house, and when thou walkest by the way; and when thou liest down, and when thou risest up"
(Deuteronomy 6:6,7).

Project One

☐ Discuss some of the ways in which the world has perverted the concepts of romantic relationships.

DATE ATTEMPTED: _____

RESULTS: _____

_____

_____

Project Two

☐ Discuss words such as "love", "romance", "commitment", "marriage", etc. and how these words have been changed or confused by the world.

DATE ATTEMPTED: _____

RESULTS: _____

_____

_____

Project Three

☐ Spend time with your young people evaluating their relationships, and setting moral and spiritual standards for dating.

DATE ATTEMPTED: _____

RESULTS: _____

_____

_____

30

Guidelines for Dating

SCRIPTURE READING: II Timothy 2:19-22; I Timothy 4:12-5:2

After having viewed God's perspective in the area of dating and relating to the opposite sex, we want to apply these principles in a practical way for the sake of those parents and young people who are presently facing these important decisions.

WHAT ARE SOME GUIDELINES FOR PARENTS IN HELPING THEIR YOUNG PEOPLE PROPERLY RELATE TO OTHERS OF THE OPPOSITE SEX?

• Parents should always prayerfully consider any relationship at any age in the light of God's present and future will for their son or daughter (see lesson 28).

• Parents should work with their children from school age years upward in helping them discern character qualities in their friends, such as:

- Commitment to God *(II Corinthians 6:14-18)*
- Attitude toward authority *(Proverbs 13:20)*
- Honestly, truthfulness *(Ephesians 5:11-12)* ·
- Faithfulness *(Proverbs 20:6)*
- Meekness, ability to control anger *(Proverbs 22:24-25)*

• Parents should always make judgments in relation to this area keeping in mind what is best for their son or daughter, rather than their own personal interests.

• Parents must avoid the temptation of trying to relive their lives through their young people.

• Parents should take the initiative in limiting or breaking off any relationships of their child with another which is in any way detracting from their son's or daughter's success — whether spiritually, academically, or socially.

- Thoroughly communicate your feelings and convictions to your son or daughter, expressing your love, understanding, and concern.

- When possible, discuss the situation with the other parents involved, being careful not to be judgmental of their child.

- Give special attention to your child during this time, realizing you must replace that which you have taken away. Use this as an opportunity to grow closer to your own son or daughter.

WHAT SPECIFIC GUIDELINES SHOULD PARENTS GIVE TO THEIR YOUNG PEOPLE FOR RELATING TO THE OPPOSITE SEX?

• Young people should have clear guidelines for their social activities.

• When should they be home? Set a specific curfew.
• With whom are they going?
• Where are they going?
• What will they be doing?
• Who is responsible? Who is chaperoning?
• Who is driving or providing transportation?

• Young people should be encouraged to develop wholesome relationships with many other growing Christian young people in:

• Brother/sister relationships
• Sincere friendships
• Wholesome Christian group activities
• Church functions

• Teens in high school should be discouraged from any steady romantic relationships. An emotional focus on one person causes many problems:

• Neglect of other people, friends, responsibilities and spiritual life
• Stunted spiritual, emotional, and social development
• Loss of other needed relationships
• Communication barriers with others (including parents)
• Early marriage (either forced or gone into without proper preparation and maturity)

• Young people should have a clear understanding of God's moral standards and principles of godly relationships and a level of discernment to avoid the world's ways. (See lesson 29).

It is vitally important for both parents and youth to realize the differences between God's ways and other ways of approaching this sensitive area of concern. Though others do it differently or though we, as parents, had our ways of approaching dating when we were young, God's ways is the best. We must all answer to God as to how we implemented His principles in our own lives and the lives of our children.

• FAMILY PROJECTS •

SECTION 5
LESSON 30
"Guidelines for Dating"

"And these words which I command thee this day, shall be in thine heart: And thou shalt teach them diligently unto thy children and shalt talk of them when thou sittest in thine house, and when thou walkest by the way; and when thou liest down, and when thou risest up"
(Deuteronomy 6:6,7).

Project One
☐ Have a discussion between you and your mate, evaluating how well you are guiding your son or daughter in their relationships with others, particularly of the opposite sex.

DATE ATTEMPTED: _____

RESULTS: _____

_____

_____

Project Two
☐ Discuss with your teenager the negative results of steady romantic relationships and how to relate discretely with all Christian brothers and sisters.

DATE ATTEMPTED: _____

RESULTS: _____

_____

_____

_____

DATE ATTEMPTED: _____

RESULTS: _____

_____

_____

31

Dating and Engagement

SCRIPTURE READING: Proverbs 18:22; 31:11-31;
I Thessalonians 4:2-8

There is hardly an area of life in which godly wisdom is needed more than for romantic relationships. In the last number of years there has been a great effort made to apply Biblical wisdom to marriage. It is our desire to see the same effort made concerning the romantic relationships that lead to marriage.

WHAT IS A STEADY DATING RELATIONSHIP?

It is the development of a romantic relationship based upon a solid friendship, guided by the ways of God, and headed toward a possible marriage choice. To avoid the abuse of romance and selfish exploitation, a dating relationship should always be viewed as exploring a possible marriage choice. This will involve getting to know a person well enough in a romantic relationship to be able to make a wise and solid marriage commitment. This cannot be done from a distance. There must be a considerable amount of personal involvement, time, and shared experienced to make this knowledge both substantial and realistic. Scripture seems to encourage exploring a marriage choice: "Whoso findeth a wife

findeth a good thing . . ." *(Proverbs 18:22)*. "Who can find a virtuous woman?" *(Proverbs 31:10)*

WHAT CONCEPTS SHOULD FORM THE BASIS FOR A DATING RELATIONSHIP?

- Friendship should be developed before romance.

- A romantic relationship will arise out of a lifestyle of serving others and of developing a full range of successful friendships.

- Romantic interest should be developed with only one person at a time.

- The possibility of a marriage choice should temper all romantic relationships. You should not be dating someone you would not consider to be a potential marriage partner.

- For wisdom and safety, a romantic relationship should be under natural (parental) and spiritual (pastoral) covering.

- All decisions must be submitted to the witness of godly wisdom and right timing.

• A relationship should be developed slowly and naturally.

HOW SHOULD A ROMANTIC RELATIONSHIP BEGIN?

It should begin with a joint decision to allow a romantic relationship to develop, based on an established friendship, honest communication, and mutual desires. A romance is to be a communicated, mutual decision for the sake of commitment and a sense of responsibility. The following are elements that should be considered in the decision to develop a healthy, romantic relationship:

• Evaluate the past and present relationship. How strong is it? How well do we know each other? How well do we communicate? What fruit have we seen in our friendship? Good? Bad? Spiritual? Carnal?

• Determine if there is a mutual desire to develop a romantic relationship. If there isn't, there is no need to proceed any further.

• Consider the time element. Is it the right time? Is the relationship ready for a romantic element?

• Make the decision a matter of prayerful consideration. What does God think about it?

• Hold the decision tentatively until it has been submitted to your covering for counsel. The fellow should ask the girl's father or covering for permission to begin a romantic relationship.

• Together, submit the relationship to God. Yield your rights to each other to Him, and confirm your accountability to Him for what you contribute to the relationship.

• Set your mutual dating standards by combining your individual ones and determining to live by the stricter.

• Make sure the following mutual commitments are clear:
  • NO commitment to marriage. This commitment should never be assumed before engagement.
  • Commitment to guard one's own feelings
  • Commitment to protect the other persons' feelings
  • Commitment to communicate honestly and openly
  • Commitment to submit the relationship and possible marriage decision to the Lord

WHAT PRINCIPLES SHOULD GOVERN A DATING RELATIONSHIP?

SUBMISSION TO GOD

All our desires, values, actions, thoughts and decisions must be yielded to the Lord. His will must be sought. It is when we take things out of His hands that we run the risk of serious mistakes.

COVERING

Seeking the counsel and confirmation of those over us is a practical way of measuring our responsiveness to God's authority. It also helps protect us from unwise decisions.

RESPONSIBILITY

Recognizing that God holds us accountable for how we relate to others, we must act responsibly in the relationship and avoid allowing it to wander aimlessly.

COMMITMENT

We must remain loyal to the other person as a brother or sister in Christ, whether or not the relationship leads to marriage.

SENSITIVITY

Being constantly considerate of the needs, opinions, and values of the other person will release us from being overly concerned about our own.

EXPECTATIONS

Your expectations of the other person must be yielded to God. Expectations are caused by seeking to receive, desiring others to meet your needs and focusing on how someone can please you. If two people are primarily looking for someone to meet their needs, their relationship will lead to a marriage in which they are merely trying to get something from each other. *Luke 6:27-45* deals with this attitude. Personal gain is a byproduct of serving others. We must channel our sense of need into meeting others' needs. The only legitimate concern for our personal needs is for God's purposes in our lives *(James 4:3)*. Our first concern should be how we can benefit their life and secondly how they can benefit ours.

CONTROL

The emotional level of the relationship should be monitored by regulating the level of time, words and actions that are shared together.

TIMING

The relationship should be allowed to grow naturally without moving too quickly. Though the relationship should not be left dormant, the test of time should be allowed to be its greatest witness.

MUTUALITY

The two involved should grow together in the relationship without racing ahead of each other. It would not be healthy for it to become unequal in commitment nor emotionally imbalanced.

LOVE

Have the other person's best interests in mind at all times.

KNOWLEDGE

Recognize that mental knowledge of another person does not constitute the reality of a relationship; only personal knowledge that comes through sharing experiences of life together.

COMMUNICATION

Promote interpersonal understanding and commitment by an honest and meaningful interchange on a wide range of areas, not just talking about "us" all of the time.

WHAT AREAS IN EACH OTHER'S LIVES SHOULD BE CONSIDERED IN MAKING A MARRIAGE CHOICE?

Spiritual Life

When considering a potential mate, one should give primary consideration to their relationship to God, including the strength of their personal commitment, ability to flow together in spiritual things, involvement in prayer and the Word, and spiritual growth and witness.

Personal Life

A persons's character qualities, personality traits, habit patterns and ability to change, should be considered.

Social Life

Much insight can be gained from a persons's interpersonal relationships. Apart from your own relationship to them, you should take into account their relationship to their parents, the church, their friends and family, as well as their ability to communicate, to handle irritations, to resolve conflicts, and their social fluidity and response to authority.

Natural Life

Also to be considered are a person's age, education, domestic life, work stability, financial freedom, and recreational interests.

Vocational Life

Attention should be given to career direction, ministry direction, purposefulness, goals, and flexibility, especially to discern whether these areas are compatible with yours.

HOW SHOULD ENGAGEMENT BE HANDLED?

The purpose of engagement is to provide a bridge from the state of being single to the state of being married. This is based on the recognition that this change will affect and involve many people, and that this adjustment will take some time to take place smoothly.

- Engagement begins with the couple's mutual commitment to marry, which should include their consulting with their parental and pastoral coverings before the decision is finalized. Parental blessings should be viewed as being a necessary confirmation of the marriage choice.

- A public announcement and an engagement ring are external signs of the internal choice and attest to the genuineness of the commitment.

- The length of the engagement should be deermined by a consideration of the following:

  - The time needed to make necessary arrangements for the wedding
  - Family and friends having enough time to prepare for the wedding
  - The groom's financial status
  - Special considerations such as job or schooling

- Though all doubts should be dealt with before an engagement is made, it should not be viewed as being entirely irrevocable. On the other hand, engagement should not be considered as a time of deciding whether or not to marry someone. Engagement is a serious promise to marry.

32

Marriage, Divorce, Remarriage and Reconciliation

SCRIPTURE READING: *Hebrews 13:4; Malachi 2:16; Deuteronomy 24:1-4; Matthew 5:31,32; Matthew 19:4-12; Luke 16:18; Mark 10:2-12; I Corinthians 7:10-16*

This lesson is intended to be a simple, basic outline of our view on the subject of marriage, divorce, remarriage, and reconciliation. It is NOT intended to answer all the questions to this complex subject. Since this subject is so enshrouded with emotions, you must be cautioned that any conclusions you form as a result of this lesson (since the lesson is not discussed in its entirety) may be incomplete, inaccurate, or not in accord with the full view of the leadership of this church. Any questions you have regarding these issues you should direct to your elder. This will enable us all to avoid unnecessary misunderstanding and flow together in one mind and spirit in the Body.

OBJECTIVES OF THIS LESSON:

- Informative — to make the members of the Body aware of this local church's view on this subject.

- Preventative — to underscore the permanence, solemnity, and finality of the marriage bond.

- Restorative — to offer mercy, comfort, and strength to those who live under condemnation as a result of divorce.

DEFINITIONS:

- **Marriage** is the contractual, binding commitment to live together in a relationship recognized morally by God and society, enacted verbally, validated legally, and consummated physically.

- **Divorce** is the breaking and forsaking of the marriage contract and all of its moral, legal, and physical obligations.

- **Valid Remarriage** is entering into a new marriage contract by or with someone who has been formerly married but is not now in **ANY** way bound to the former partner or partners in some sort of marital obligation (those obligations having been dissolved through death or remarriage on the part of the former spouse or spouses).

- **Reconciliation** is the process of saying and doing the things necessary to restore and reunite a couple into the relationship that God wants them to have (spiritually and/or physically).

WHAT IS GOD'S VIEWPOINT OF MARRIAGE?

Genesis 2:24,25; Hebrews 13:4; I Corinthians 7:10,12,15; Mark 10:9; I Peter 3:7

- Marriage is a part of God's design for relationship between opposite sexes.

- Marriage is a commitment ("cleaving") that binds two people together in a special relationship of love and mutual sharing. The Hebrew meaning for the word "cleave" here means "to glue together."

- Marriage is blessed, sanctified, and exalted by God.

- Marriage in God's mind is a permanent situation. God never intended that people should ever consider divorce as an option to an unhappy marriage *(Mark 10:4-9)*. Marriage is a covenant or "contract" between a man and a woman to be held inviolable by both.

WHAT IS THE BIBLICAL VIEWPOINT OF DIVORCE?

- In the beginning, God intended that the marriage bond be permanent *(Genesis 2:24-25)*.

- Under the law, Moses permitted divorce for specified reasons though the underlying cause was hardness of heart *(Exodus 21:7-11; Deuteronomy 21:10-14; Deuteronomy 24:1-4; Matthew 19:7,8)*.

- Under the prophets, God clearly stated that He hated divorce and that it was a reproach to His name *(Malachi 2:14-16; Micha 2:9; Jeremiah 3:1)*.

- In the Gospels, Jesus clearly stated that whoever divorces for any cause, except fornication, commits adultery if they marry another, and the new partner who marries them is also guilty of adultery *(Matthew 19:3-12)*. It should be clearly understood in Jesus' statement that "what God hath joined together, let no man put asunder" is a very serious statement about the permanence of the marriage covenant.

- In the Epistles, Paul to the Corinthians makes a clear command that husbands or wives are not to divorce their respective mates *(I Corinthians 7:10-12)*.

Summary on Divorce

The Bible makes a clear statement that God's viewpoint underscores the permanence of the marriage vow with the strongest emphasis possible *(Matthew 19:10)*. Divorce is not an option to be considered, even in the face of great unhappiness. Jesus only allows for one possible cause for divorce, and that is adultery. Even with this tremendous strain upon the marriage, the highest goal is to forgive, and reconstruct a God-honoring relationship.

COULD ONE DIVORCE HIS/HER SPOUSE FOR ADULTERY AND STILL BE GUILTY OF HARDNESS OF HEART?

Yes. To be legitimate in one's actions does not automatically mean one's attitude is right. To use divorce as a punishment or a means of exacting revenge is just the heart attitude that Jesus condemns. To forgive and be reconciled would go much further in advancing the kingdom of God as well as healing the inner wounds of both parties. Many times (though not all) the "innocent" party has directly on indirectly contributed to the adultery on the part of the mate. This can rarely be determined by the "innocent" party. To divorce under such a circumstance would surely constitute hardness of heart *(Matthew 19:8)*.

IS DIVORCE (WHICH CONSTITUTES THE BREAKING OF A COVENANT) A FORGIVABLE SIN?

If one initiates a wrongful divorce and later genuinely recognizes the error of his way and sincerely repents, he has the full assurance of God's Word that he is forgiven. The Bible makes it clear that only one sin is unpardonable, namely blasphemy against the Holy Ghost *(Matthew 12:31,32)*. No Bible scholar will assert that divorce is the unpardonable sin. Thus divorce, a sin like any other sin, is washed away by the blood of Jesus, ie taken by God from the record of sins recorded never to be raised in this life or at the judgment day. We should forgive ourselves and others who have found themselves in this state, even as God forgives us *(Ephesians 4:32)*.

The consequences of the sin of divorce, however, may not be able to be undone. Like many other sins, the law of reaping tragically exacts its toll in the memory and the circumstances as one watches the seeds of a broken home harvested. This can only be met by the sustaining endurance found only in the depths of the grace and mercy of God.

WHAT DO THE SCRIPTURES SAY ABOUT REMARRIAGE?

There is very little direct reference to the concept of remarriage in the Scriptures, but several passages allude to it indirectly.

- Remarriage under the law of Moses was an understood privilege, just as divorce was liberally granted *(Exodus 21:7-10; Deuteronomy 24:1-4)*. The High Priest could not marry a divorced woman but others could *(Leviticus 21:14)*.

- Moses makes it clear that the remarriage of one who is divorced prevents him from ever returning to the original partner. The original partner, since there can be no reconciliation, is free from any marital obligation to the original spouse and thus is free to remarry *(Deuteronomy 24:1-4)*.

- In the Gospels, Jesus ays that whoever divorces because of the adultery committed by their spouse would not be committing adultery if they (the "innocent party") remarried *(Matthew 19:9)*. However, they might be guilty of hardness of heart.

- Paul makes remarriage clear in the Epistles when he states that death is the thing that finally, ultimately, and absolutely dissolves the marriage contract. The living partner is free to remarry or marry again without condemnation *(Romans 7:1-3)*. The death of one partner ends all of the marital obligations of the other partner.

Summary of remarriage

A valid remarriage is one that fits the following criteria:

- When one partner dies, it leaves the other free to remarry.

- When one partner divorces and wrongfully remarries it leaves the other partner legitimately free to remarry since there can be no reconciliation *(Deuteronomy 24:1-4)*.

- When one partner divorces his/her partner who has committed adultery, and the adulterer remarries, the other partner legitimately is free to remarry.

Remarriage is a very serious undertaking, because it is, once again, a solemn vow to remain with the new partner as long as both live. It should only be entered into with real caution and counsel in order not to repeat the mistakes of former relationships.

WHAT IS THE BIBLICAL BASIS FOR RECONCILIATION?

- The general principle of reconciliation in broken relationships applies to any and all who have become estranged in some form or another from soneome else *(Matthew 18:15-35; Ephesians 4:25-32)*.

- Specifically in the matter of divorce, Paul says that divorced partners should remain unmarried or be reconciled *(I Corinthians 7:10,11)*. If one marries following divorce, there can be no reconciliation to the marriage and, therefore, the mistake of divorce cannot be rectified *(Deuteronomy 24:1-4)*. The honor of God's name is at stake in the divorce of two believers. Every effort must be taken to preserve God'shonor (at the very least in reconciliation) as a testimony to the world that Christians are fully able to keep their word to God and to each other.

WHAT IS MEANT BY RECONCILIATION?

There are two basic kinds of reconciliation: spiritual and geographical.

- Spiritual reconciliation is the process that two estranged, divorced, or separated people take to resolve the resentments, the unforgiven sins, and the divisive attitudes that have separated them *(Matthew 18:15-35; Ephesians 4:25-32)*. To fail to be reconciled is to give Satan further advantage to reproach the name of God. Thus, this type of reconciliation should even take place between a believer and an unbeliever, as much as it is possible, to enable the believer to reinstate his Christian witness if it is tarnished, to rid himself of grace-denying guilt, and to give the unbeliever an opportunity to accept Christ as personal Savior, even if the estranged parties never reunite geographically. This type of reconciliation should always be attempted *(Romans 12:18)*.

- Geographical reconciliation occurs in the process of spiritual reconciliation. The estranged couple, in recognizing the error of their way, choose to forgive each other, repent of their sins, and move back together into the same dwelling.

SHOULD GEOGRAPHICAL RECONCILIATION EVER NOT BE SOUGHT?

Yes. If one partner has remarried, geographical reconciliation should definitely not be sought *(Deuteronomy 24:1-4)*. Or, if one partner has remarried, and their spouse dies or divorces them, they should not seek geographical reconciliation with the original spouse *(Deuteronomy 24:1-4)*.

WHY IS THE TRUTH OF RECONCILIATION SO IMPORTANT TO BELIEVERS?

- It enables married or formerly married partners to break the power of sin and bitterness in their lives *(James 4:4-10; Hebrews 12:12-17)*.

- It reinstates the testimony of the Church of Jesus Christ in an age of covenant-breaking *(II Timothy 3:3)*.

- It underscores and reemphasizes the permanence of the marriage bond *(Matthew 19:6,10)*.

- It testifies to the ability of the grace of God to conquer all human obstacles *(Hebrews 12:15)*.

33

SECTION V — SPECIAL RELATIONSHIPS IN THE FAMILY

The Single Parent

SCRIPTURE READING: Deuteronomy 14:28,29; 24:17-22; 26:12-15

WHY IS THIS AREA OF SINGLE PARENTHOOD SO IMPORTANT TODAY?

It is so important because in the United States approximately one fourth of all households with children area headed by single parents, and the number of single parent homes is growing at a rate almost three times faster than two parent homes. If the church is going to minister effectively to this rapidly growing segment of society, it must equip itself with love and understanding.

WHO IS THE SINGLE PARENT?

- Those adults who alone bear the principal responsibility for the care and raising of a child.

- Traditionally, most single parents have been women. However, the number of men who are single parents is increasing rapidly.

- Most have become single parents by way of marriage and divorce. The pressures on these homes are perhaps the greatest and most complex, including custody rights, visitation privileges, child support, emotional tension, and misunderstanding.

- Those who become parents outside of marriage also face special pressures. For example, pressures accompanying pre-marital pregnancy often include abortion, adoption, and marriage vs. no marriage.

- Some become single parents by the death of their mate, thus facing the pain of an undesired and permanent loss.

- Now a growing number of singles are adopting children by themselves, the impact of which is yet to be fully felt.

- Though admittedly disadvantaged, single parents must be respected as being able, through the grace of God and the loving concern of others, to raise their children successfully.

HOW DOES GOD VIEW SINGLE PARENTS AND THEIR CHILDREN?

The best way to discover this is to consider what the

Bible teaches concerning widows and the fatherless. Principles drawn from these passages can be applied to almost all single parent families. According to Strong's Concordance the root definition of the Hebrew word for widow may also include a divorced woman. The following Scriptures illustrate the fact that God has a special, loving concern for single parent families and wants His people to share this concern.

- They are under God's care *(Psalm 10:14; 68:5,6; 146:9; Proverbs 15:25; Hosea 14:3).*

- They are under His covering and protection *(Deuteronomy 10:18; Psalm 82:3; Jeremiah 49:11).*

- God commands others to help them and never to take advantage of them *(Deuteronomy 24:17; Isaiah 1:17; Jeremiah 7:6; 22:3; Zechariah 7:9,10; I Timothy 5:3; James 1:27).*

- God will judge those who oppress them *(Exodus 22:22-24; Deuteronomy 27:19; Proverbs 23:10,11).*

WHAT ARE SOME OF THE SPECIAL NEEDS AND PROBLEMS THAT SINGLE PARENTED FAMILIES FACE?

- Loneliness and a lack of fellowship for both parent and child.

- The need for acceptance because of the sense of being out of place around both single adults and married couples.

- The lack of covering and counsel.

- Financial lack and pressure.

- Children lacking the influence of the other parent.

- Insecurity in the children due to a lack of parental oversight and too much babysitting.

- Child discipline problems.

- Children developing a wrong view of men or women, either harboring resentment or overly desiring their attention.

WHAT SHOULD A SINGLE PARENT DO ABOUT THESE NEEDS?

- Make their relationship to the Lord top priority so that He can fulfill the role of the missing parent in that home *(I Timothy 5:5).*

- Learn to trust in the Lord and submit their expectations, needs, and desires to Him. This will free them from an overdependency on people *(Jeremiah 49:11).*

- Reestablish their relationship to their natural family, if possible, for the sake of covering and support *(I Timothy 5:4,8,16; Leviticus 22:13).*

- Do all they can to meet the needs of others *(I Timothy 5:10).*

- Identify themselves with a strong family *(Psalm 68:5,6).*

WHAT IS THE CHURCH'S RESPONSIBILITY TO SINGLE FAMILIES?

- To provide loving acceptance, Biblical counsel, and practical assistance

- The leadership of the church should provide a spiritual covering for them.

- The deacons of the church should provide practical covering *(Acts 6:1-3).*

- The families of the church should provide supplemental covering and open homes.

HOW CAN THE FAMILIES OF THE CHURCH HELP SINGLE PARENTS?

- By sharing family activities with them, including family nights, outings, and holidays

- Financial assistance

- Spending time with their children to help fill the vacuum of the missing parent

- Practical help in areas they are not capable

- Child care

- Help with canning and food storage

- Transportation

34

SECTION VI — THE MINISTRY OF THE FAMILY

Hospitality in the Home

SCRIPTURE READING: Genesis 18:1-8; Proverbs 9:1-6

Once our homes are operating under God's rule and authority, God wants every Christian home to be a place of ministry to others. In the New Testament, the home was a very important place for the cultivation of Christian fellowship and the manifestation of Christian virtues. Christianity did not only find expression in the temple, but it continued from house to house *(Acts 2:46; 5:42)*. One of the best ways that a Christian family can minister from their home is in the area of hospitality.

WHAT DOES THE WORD "HOSPITALITY" MEAN?

There are several words in our language that help to shed light on this subject.

- **Hospitable:** Disposed to behave in a warm manner or to entertain with generous kindness.

- **Hospital:** An institution for the reception, care, and medical treatment of the sick or wounded. Formerly, a place of hospitality for those in need of shelter and care.

- **Hospitality:** The spirit, practice, or act of being hospitable. In the New Testament the Greek word that is used for hospitality is made up of two words and literally means "a love of strangers". True hospitality, therefore, has nothing to do with the entertaining of friends, although that is an important aspect of Christian fellowship. True hospitality involves extending your love with warmth and generosity to those you do not know *(I Timothy 5:10)*, to those who have very definite needs, and to those who need to have their wounds bound up. Consider the good Samaritan *(Luke 10:30-37)*.

WHAT DOES THE BIBLE TEACH ABOUT HOSPITALITY IN THE OLD AND NEW TESTAMENTS?

- Hospitality is considered a requirement among the people of God in both the Old and New Testaments *(Leviticus 19:10, 33-34; I Peter 4:9)*.

  - It is expected that God's people will have sympathy on others because they, too, were once strangers *(Exodus 22:21; 23:9)*.
  - It is expected that God's people will render this service without complaint or neglect *(Hebrews 13:1-3; I Peter 4:9)*. It should be done joyfully.

- It is expected that God's people would be willing to treat a stranger the same way they would treat a friend *(Leviticus 24:22; Deuteronomy 27:19).*

- Hospitality is a prerequisite for all those who want to lead, guide, and serve God's people.

  - All leadership had to be an example in this area *(I Timothy 3:2; Titus 1:7-8).*
  - Widows had to possess this quality to be on the widow's roll *(I Timothy 5:10).*

- Hospitality is a means whereby a wise person will lead others into the understanding of truth *(Proverbs 9:1-6).*

WHO ARE SOME BIBLICAL ILLUSTRATIONS OF THIS MINISTRY?

There are many examples of hospitality in the Bible. Some examples are good and some are bad.

- On the negative side, we can see how strongly the spirit of hospitality was ingrained in the thinking of God's people by the way in which negative examples were handled.

  - Gibeah refused to extend hospitality *(Judges 19:15).* Eventually, the entire tribe of Benjamin was judged as a result *(Judges 20).*
  - Nabal almost lost his life when he refused to show hospitality to David *(I Samuel 25:10-11).*
  - Jethro was astonished when his daughters did not invite Moses to stay with them *(Exodus 2:20).*
  - James and John were ready to call down fire from heaven at the lack of hospitality they experienced by the Samaritans *(Luke 9:51-56).*

- On the positive side, we have many that showed a true spirit of hospitality.

  - Lot constrained the two angels to spend the night *(Genesis 19:1-11).*
  - Rahab protected the spies from hurt in her home *(Joshua 2:1-16).*
  - David extended his royal table to Mephibosheth *(II Samuel 9:1-13).*
  - The widow at Zarephath extended sacrificial hospitality to Elijah *(I Kings 17:8-16).*
  - The only woman called "great" in the Bible was a woman of hospitality *(II Kings 4:8-17).*
  - One of the best examples is Abraham's treatment of the three strangers who appeared to him *(Genesis 18:1-8).* Notice the actions of Abraham:

    - He bows to the ground.
    - He prays them to stay.
    - He gave them rest.
    - He washed their feet.
    - He fed them and gave them drink.
    - He verbally identified himself as their servant.
    - He hurried in serving them.
    - He gave them the best of everything.

- There are many New Testament examples as well:

    - Martha to Jesus *(Luke 10:38)*
    - Zaccheus to Jesus *(Luke 19:5-6)*
    - Lydia to Paul and Silas *(Acts 16:15)*
    - Publius to Paul *(Acts 28:7)*
    - Onesiphorus to Paul *(II Timothy 1:16)*
    - Simon, the tanner, to Peter *(Acts 10:32)*

WHAT DOES IT COST TO GET INVOLVED IN THE MINISTRY OF HOSPITALITY?

Hospitality will involve a spirit of generosity in several areas.

- It will cost financially.

- It will involve giving up some privacy.

- It will involve a sacrifice of time and energy.

- It will involve laying down personal desires for the benefit of others.

The ministry of hospitality is a ministry that God wants to give to every member of the Body of Christ *(Romans 12:13).* It is a ministry that has its own rewards because whatever is done to the least of the brethren is done to Christ, and Christ is a debtor to no man *(Matthew 25:35).*

WHAT IS THE BASIC ATTITUDE OR MOTIVATION BEHIND TRUE BIBLICAL HOSPITALITY?

The main motivation behind this ministry is that of sacrificial love *(I Corinthians 13:3).* God has given to us freely. We are to give freely to others *(Matthew 10:8).*

Hospitality is to be extended to those who have definite needs which you have the ability to meet *(I John 3:16-18).* The New Testament teaches that we are to extend hospitality to:

- Traveling ministry *(III John 5-6)*

- Saints *(I Peter 4:9)*

- Out-of-towners *(III John 5-6)*

- Newcomers *(Hebrews 13:1-2)*

- The poor, lame, blind, or all those who cannot repay *(Hebrews 13:1-2; Luke 14:12-14; Matthew 22:2-10)*

God wants this ministry to be especially given in a sacrificial way to those who have no ability to repay the kindness *(Luke 14:14).*

WHAT IS THE PRIMARY PURPOSE OF BIBLICAL HOSPITALITY?

God wants to use the ministry of the home as a base to reach out to others who have definite needs. In reaching out in this manner, the Christian family has an opportunity to:

- Meet the real physical needs of people
- Share the truth of the gospel
- Demonstrate other Christian virtues
- Reach out in counsel, comfort, and encouragement

• FAMILY PROJECTS •

SECTION 6
LESSON 34
"Hospitality in the Home"

"And these words which I command thee this day, shall be in thine heart: And thou shalt teach them diligently unto thy children and shalt talk of them when thou sittest in thine house, and when thou walkest by the way; and when thou liest down, and when thou risest up"
(Deuteronomy 6:6,7).

Project One   ☐   Have a family discussion in which you discuss the definitions give in Question #1 of the lesson. Ask the question, "How well do we measure our home against the definitions?" and, "What do you think we could do to improve?"

DATE ATTEMPTED: _____

RESULTS: _____

_____

_____

Project Two   ☐   Invite someone from the church that you do not know very well over to your house for an evening. In a family discussion, plan the activities and the menu for the evening, let each family member take part in some area of service that night.

DATE ATTEMPTED: _____

RESULTS: _____

_____

_____

_____

DATE ATTEMPTED: _____

RESULTS: _____

_____

_____

35

The Ministry of the Family

God has a definite purpose and goal in all of His dealings with us as individuals and as families. God deals with us to bring us to maturity so that we might in turn reach out to others. God remakes and reshapes our lives so that we can become effective instruments in His hand for the evangelization, growth, and development of the lost and struggling of this world. God's vision is bigger than an individual. God's vision is bigger than a family or even a particular church. God's vision is for the world *(John 3:16)*. God has extended His salvation to us that we can, in turn, reach out to others.

WHAT IS THE BASIC REASON WHY GOD BLESSES HIS PEOPLE WITH ABUNDANCE AND TRUTH?

God operates on a very simple principle. He blesses us to be a blessing.

- He did this with Abraham *(Genesis 12:1-3)*.

- He did this with the children of Israel *(Isaiah 43:8-13)*.

- He does this with everyone *(II Corinthians 1:3-4; I Timothy 6:17-19)*.

WHAT IS THE RESPONSIBILITY OF GOD'S PEOPLE WHO HAVE BEEN BLESSED WITH TRUTH?

In response to what God has done, God expects His people to be willing to reach out to others. God has established His people as a royal priesthood *(Exodus 19:4-6; I Peter 2:5-9)*. As a priesthood we are to:

- Be a servant nation to the world *(Isaiah 49:3-6; Acts 1:8)*

- Mediate the blessing of God to the rest of the earth *(Exodus 19:5)*

- Live in the "environment of God" while living in the midst of the nations, thus showing forth His glory *(Matthew 5:13-16)*

- Be God's vehicle to show forth God's praises to the world *(Isaiah 43:21; I Peter 2:9)*

- Be witnesses to the world of the power and love of God *(Isaiah 44:8; 43:9-12; Acts 1:8)*

WHAT PLACE DOES THE HOME HAVE IN REACHING OUT TO OTHERS?

The Bible teaches that a home that is in order can become a real place of manifold ministry. In the New Testament the home was:

- A place of refreshment *(Acts 10:6)*

- A place where the believers gathered for prayer *(Acts 12:12)*

- A place where bread was broken *(Acts 2:46)*

- A place of teaching and preaching *(Acts 5:42; 20:20)*

- A place where the Spirit was outpoured *(Acts 2:2)*

- A place where churches were started *(Acts 18:7,11; Romans 16:5; I Corinthians 16:19; Colossians 4:15; Philemon 2)*

HOW DOES GOD WANT TO USE OUR HOMES?

- God wants every home to be a place where the principles of the kingdom of God are lived out. Each home should be a showcase for Christian living. In this way our homes will become:

  - A pattern of good works attracting the lost *(Titus 2:7-8)*

  - A testimony to those who are outside the Church *(II Corinthians 8:21; I Timothy 3:7; Acts 22:12)*

  - A place where people will come for answers *(I Peter 3:15-16)*

  - A true manifestation of the wisdom of God *(Colossians 4:5; Ephesians 3:10; James 3:13)*

- God wants every home to be a place from which we can reach out to our neighborhoods. God gives us all specific duties that we are to fulfill toward our neighbors.

  - We are to love our neighbors as ourselves *(Matthew 5:43; 19:19; 22:39; Mark 12:31,33; Romans 13:9-10; James 2:8; Galatians 5:14).*
  - We are to try to please them *(Romans 15:2).*
  - We are to deal honestly with them *(Ephesians 4:25).*
  - We are to be instrumental in teaching them *(Hebrews 8:11).*

- God wants every home to be stretching out and reaching out for the poor and needy *(Proverbs 31:20).*

  - This starts with the needy in one's own and relatives *(I Timothy 5:4,8,16).*
  - This extends to the other members of the Body of Christ *(I Corinthians 16:15; Galatians 6:10; I Thessalonians 5:15).*
  - This reaches beyond to the stranger outside *(Galatians 6:10; I Thessalonians 5:15).*

WHO ARE SOME GOOD BIBLICAL EXAMPLES OF THIS KIND OF MINISTRY?

- The virtuous woman was one who always kept a candle burning in her window to guide the wayfarer to a place of shelter *(Proverbs 31:18).*

- Elizabeth had a close relationship with not only her kindred but also all of her neighbors *(Luke 1:39-45, 56-58, 15:6-9).*

- Stephanas serves as one of the best examples. Many commentators believe that this man was the Phillipian jailor converted under the ministry of Paul.

  - He was a man who was personally responsive to the Lord *(Acts 16:30-31).*
  - He was a man who immediately got his own home in order *(Acts 16:32-33; I Corinthians 1:16).*

- He was a man who was reaching out to the needs of others *(Acts 16:34).*
- He was a man who became addicted to the ministry of the saints *(I Corinthians 16:15).*
- He became a great help and strength to the apostle Paul *(I Corinthians 16:16-17).*
- He even helped pen the letter to the Corinthians *(I Corinthians — subscription).*

WHAT ARE SOME PRACTICAL WAYS IN WHICH WE CAN GET MORE ACTIVELY INVOLVED IN OUTREACH FROM OUR HOMES?

There are many things that we can do as believers. The following are only a few suggestions. You can add to your own to the list.

- Housing needy singles, whether they be newly converted or in need of local parental oversight.

- Reaching out to the older people in the Body and your neighborhood.

- Establishing a healthy relationship with your neighbors.

  - Take time to get to know them.
  - Help them with a project (i.e., canning, clean-up, etc.).
  - Be ready to assist in times of need.
  - Invite them to dinner.
  - Visit them when sick (and send a card).
  - Remember them on special occasions.
  - Talk to them when the occasion presents itself.
  - Invite them along on special family or church functions.
  - Be willing to help them with babysitting.

- Using your home for church functions.

  - Showers
  - Home meetings
  - Prayer meetings
  - Bible studies

- Reaching out to your boss and fellow employees.

The home is the place where true Christianity is displayed. People may question its authenticity in the Church, but when they see it in your home, they will be convinced *(I Peter 2:12-25).*

SECTION 6
LESSON 35
"The
Ministry of the Family"

"And these words which I command thee this day, shall be in thine heart: And thou shalt teach them diligently unto thy children and shalt talk of them when thou sittest in thine house, and when thou walkest by the way; and when thou liest down, and when thou risest up"
(Deuteronomy 6:6,7).

Project One   ☐   Discuss your relationship with your neighbors in a family discussion. Answer the following questions: What needs do we know that our neighbors have? What can we do to help them meet those needs?

DATE ATTEMPTED: _____

RESULTS: _____

_____

_____

Project Two   ☐   In the next few months, plan to have each of your immediate neighbors into your home for an evening of visiting. See to discover their real needs and how you can be of service to them.

DATE ATTEMPTED: _____

RESULTS: _____

_____

_____